ST. LUCIA

Travel Guide 2024

Your Ultimate Guide to Paradise - Discover, Explore, and Experience the Caribbean Gem

LOWE SANDBERG

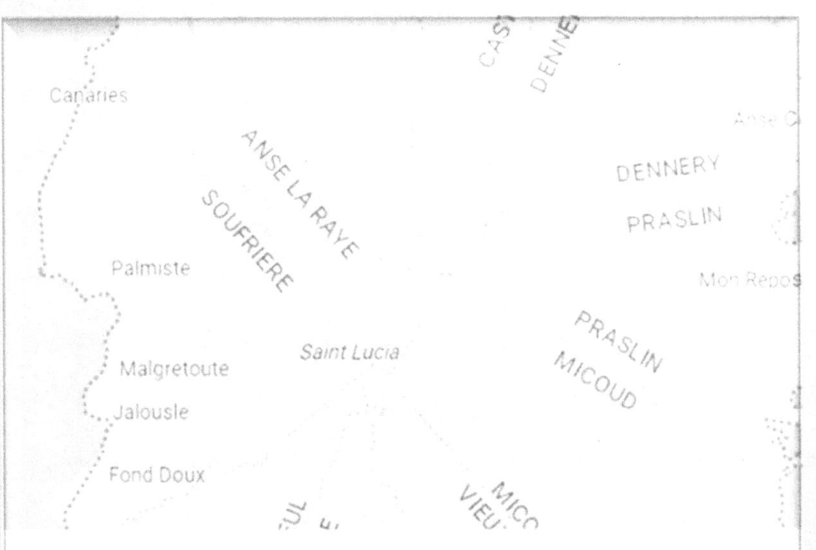

Scan QR Code with Device to View Map

Explore
ST. LUCIA

Table of Contents

Welcome to St. Lucia

St. Lucia, a beautiful Caribbean paradise, awaits your arrival. This lovely island in the eastern Caribbean Sea is well-known for its breathtaking natural beauty, lively culture, and welcoming hospitality. As you begin your trip to this tropical treasure, let us expose you to the spirit of St. Lucia, giving you a taste of what to anticipate during your stay.

Why visit St. Lucia?

Nestled amid opulent Caribbean islands like Martinique, St. Vincent, and Barbados, St. Lucia offers an exceptional blend of spectacular landscapes, lovely beaches, and rich culture. St. Lucia, which is just 40 kilometers long and 22 kilometers broad, offers guests a real Caribbean experience, allowing them to immerse themselves in a dynamic way of life while exploring the gorgeous natural surroundings. St. Lucia's complicated history currently benefits the country by blending French, African, East Indian, and English cultures, resulting in a one-of-a-kind resort that provides much more than a typical beach vacation. St. Lucia is the epitome of a wonderful island paradise.

The Pitons

The famous Pitons are among the world's most recognizable mountains. The Gros Piton and Petit Piton, towering from the ocean, stand as iconic symbols of the island, much like the Eiffel Tower represents France.

These volcanic pinnacles rise over 700 meters above sea level and are a striking feature of the St. Lucian skyline. Despite its intimidating look, Gros Piton is accessible to hikers without climbing equipment. On clear days, the summit provides breathtaking views of St. Lucia, St. Vincent, and Martinique. This UNESCO World Heritage Site reaches deep under the waves, with extensive coral reefs covering the underwater domain; the abundance of species here, both above and below the sea, is remarkable.

Beaches

Like the rest of the Caribbean, St. Lucia is often associated with white sand beaches and beautiful water. This gorgeous island has some of the most beautiful beaches in the Lesser Antilles. The magnificent Anse des Pitons, perched between the two Piton hills and with dazzling sand and towering palm palms, is the epitome of

Caribbean beach splendor. However, this is not the only notable beach on St. Lucia's coastline; Anse Chastanet, Anse Cochon, and Reduit Beach all provide magnificent tropical settings with vibrant coral reefs only a few feet from the shore, making them ideal snorkeling destinations. For turtle enthusiasts, Grande Anse is the perfect destination; from mid-March until the end of July, campers can see leatherback turtles emerge from the sea.

Sulphur Springs

A volcano in the southwestern town of Soufrière has dormant sulfur springs that have not erupted since the 1700s, yet, hot springs and mud pits remain in the region. Away from the volcano's heated core, the mud, which has several medicinal powers, is cold enough to bathe in, making it a popular tourist destination. Guests may use a beautiful waterfall nearby to rinse themselves after their sticky mud bath by letting the water from this natural jungle shower cascade 15 meters upon their heads. If you have the opportunity, a tour of the sulfur spring is a delightful way to learn more about the extraordinary history and science of this geological show while also soaking in the beauty of the breathtaking vistas.

Rainforest

St. Lucia's national rainforest, which comprises 19,000 acres of picturesque mountains and valleys, has some of the most luxuriant and brilliantly green foliage of any Caribbean island. The forest, with its amazing topography and beautiful ecosystem, is home to diverse species and flora. Visitors may see stunning wild anthurium flowers, massive gummier trees, and many other flora and animals. Hikers may see a green Iguana, a Boa Constrictor, or the fragile Jacquot, St. Lucia's national bird, hidden in the greenery. Exploring this primordial jungle is like being lost in the forest of your childhood dreams.

Diving

St. Lucia's natural wonders extend beyond the waves into underwater seascapes, resulting in the Caribbean's most colorful and scenic diving destinations. St. Lucia boasts a wealth of diving opportunities, featuring numerous top-rated PADI centers. This makes it an ideal location for divers across all skill levels to enhance their diving abilities. The most popular diving spot is located in the Soufrière Marine Reserve, where divers may explore sites such as Anse Chastanet and the Coral Gardens, as well as the artificial reefs formed by the Lesleen M and Daini Komoyaru shipwrecks. For less experienced divers, the clear waters of most of St. Lucia's beaches make it a great site to watch a variety of undersea dwellers with just a snorkel.

Soufrière

Soufrière, located on the island's west coast, is St. Lucia's ancient capital. Named by French colonists in the 1700s, its name translates to sulfur in the air and is a word used in French to characterize any volcanic terrain. This town is known as the islands' tourist hub owing to its closeness to several attractions, such as Soufrière's geothermal system, the Pitons, and the beautiful Diamond Falls. The region's wealth of French colonial buildings highlights its rich and varied past. This neighborhood embodies St. Lucia's beauty, tradition, and vibrant spirit via yearly festivals like Independence Day, Carnival, the Soufrière Creole Jazz Festival, and Christmas festivities.

History

St. Lucia's history is complicated and extensive, including important periods of colonial authority. The island's rule alternated between France and Britain over a dozen times until complete independence was attained in 1979. However, this offers St. Lucia many historical landmarks, including forts erected during the Seven Years' War and the French Revolution. St. Lucia has an exceptionally distinct history and culture, influenced by France, Africa, England, and East India. This rich past is most evident on Pigeon Island, located at the head of Rodney Bay, where Arawak and Carib artifacts dating back to 1000 A.D. may be found. Admiral George Rodney erected his well-known namesake fort on the island.

Castries

Castries, the picturesque capital of St Lucia, is located on the island's northwestern shore. The spectacular Morne Fortune Hill provides a picturesque backdrop for this capital city. Most ancient buildings were destroyed in significant fires between 1785 and 1948, but the city's bulk has been restored and retains the vibrant character of Castries' past. Its colorful structures and colonial influence may be seen throughout the city. This city is a major cruise ship port with a thriving tourism industry, including many colorful businesses and marketplaces and various notable landmarks such as the Cathedral Immaculate Conception, Derek Walcott Square, the city library, the Government House, and Fort Charlotte. This city is ideal for those who wish to experience the island's rich past.

Waterfalls

Waterfalls have an awe-inspiring quality that transports you to another realm. Fortunately, St. Lucia has some of the most stunning waterfalls in the Caribbean. Diamond Falls is one of the islands' most renowned waterfalls. This stunning sight in the Diamond Botanical Garden rises around 15 meters tall and is filled with natural minerals that give the water a vibrant shine. Other outstanding waterfalls on the island include the Sault Falls, Anse La Raye Falls, and Spyke Falls. Indeed, to immerse yourself in St. Lucia, you must visit at least one of its numerous waterfalls. The island paradise is replete with waterfalls, which have become an iconic feature of its image.

Chocolate

The 140-acre Rabot Estate is located in St. Lucia's southwest corner, surrounded by high hills and falling rainforest valleys. Notably, this is the chocolate-producing plantation for the world-renowned Hotel Chocolat. The islands' rich soil, high altitude, and rainforest water provide an ideal habitat for cocoa bean production. Hotel Chocolat also operates the boutique Boucan Hotel, which offers breathtaking views of the 250-year-old estate and the Piton Mountains. Unsurprisingly, a chocolate theme runs throughout the hotel, with tours of the cocoa trees and the possibility of manufacturing your chocolate. Rabot Estate is worth a visit. St. Lucia is certainly a chocolate lover's delight.

13 Interesting Facts About St. Lucia.

St. Lucia was the first nation named after a woman.

One of only two nations in the world named after a woman. St Lucia is named after St. Lucy of Syracuse. However, St. Lucia is the only nation named after a historical lady.

The name given by French colonizers to this place was in tribute to St. Lucy, the patron St. revered for her protection against blindness and throat diseases. It seems that St. Lucy was not initially a favored option during the allocation of patron St.s.

The island obtained independence from Britain in 1979.

Known as the "Helen of the Caribbean" since control of the island was transferred seven times between the French and the British in the 1800s. The British ultimately won out, but St Lucia attained independence in 1979 and joined the Commonwealth.

The Jacquot, or the St Lucia Parrot, is exclusively found in St Lucia.

We admit it: You probably didn't need to be Hercule Poirot to figure out where the St Lucia Parrot originated. However, this amazing bird can only be seen on the island and is the country's official bird.

St. Lucia is home to the Pitons mountain range, a UNESCO World Heritage site.

You'll probably find it hard to find a photo of St Lucia that doesn't show the beautiful Pitons. These two towering mountains offer excellent tourist attractions, extraordinary atmospheric shifts that allow species to flourish, and even inspiration for the island's beer.

It is home to the world's only "drive-in" volcano.

There is lots of volcanic activity all across St Lucia, which is also where the Pitons originated. But the Sulphur Springs are heated volcanic springs that attract people from all over the globe.

Therapeutic mud baths and various exciting activities are available, such as nature hikes and, you guessed it, a volcano to drive around.

The Roseau Valley in St Lucia is home to 21 distinct varieties of rum!

In St. Lucia, as in numerous other Caribbean regions, rum production plays a vital role in the economy. The Roseau Valley, known for its extensive banana fields, also boasts an abundance of distilleries. These facilities expertly convert the region's abundant sugar cane into exquisite rum.

During one of the plantation visits, you can manufacture your chocolate bar.

Speaking about plantations, we can't speak about St Lucia without mentioning chocolate. The Rabot Estate is one of the country's most renowned chocolate estates, supplying cocoa to businesses such as Hotel Chocolat.

When you next visit St Lucia, take a Rabot Estate plantation tour and construct your confection.

Over 70% of the island is covered by jungle.

A varied island. St Lucia offers everything from beautiful beaches to high peaks, and most of the nation is covered in lush rainforest.

Famous pirates Jambre De Bois ("Peg Leg") and Blackbeard visited the island, most likely owing to the abundance of rum!

Blackbeard is said to have hidden some wealth near Vieux Fort, a village in the island's south. Unfortunately, this was never validated. Although both vagabonds undoubtedly visited the island, there are reports of Peg Leg fighting Spanish ships from the fortification on Pigeon Island.

There are 180 kinds of birds on the island.

Scientists have also discovered six species that are unique to the island. Making St. Lucia an ultimate refuge for avarian creatures.

St. Lucia has its home-brewed pilsner, Piton.

Although there is plenty of rum in St Lucia, the residents enjoy a glass of Piton, a home-brewed spirit. The Pilsner beer, named after renowned sites, is ideal for staying cool on another scorching island day.

The Caribbean Island boasts more Nobel laureates per capita than any other nation.

The nation has two Nobel Prize winners: Sir Arthur Lewis for economics and Derek Walcott for literature, both of whom won in 1992.

St Lucia has a year-round average temperature of 27°.

Perhaps this is why we like it so much.

Chapter 1: Getting to Know St. Lucia

A Brief History.

St. Lucia's past is a vibrant mosaic. Over centuries, this island has been a crucible of diverse cultures and a portal to the Americas. As a result, the island has a strong feeling of tradition and cultural identity, which the residents celebrate to this day. Immerse yourself in St. Lucia's tale, from her colorful pirate history and colonial past to her people's firmly held traditions.

Early St. Lucia History

St. Lucia, originally named "Louanalao" by the Arawak Indians around 200 AD, translating to "Island of the Iguanas," was later renamed "Hewanorra" in 800 AD following the arrival and settlement of the Carib Indians. To this day, descendants of the Carib people continue to reside in St. Lucia.

The Caribs inhabited St. Lucia until the 1600s when immigrants sought to seize control of the island to enhance European commerce. Even throughout this age of colonialism, the Caribs continued to battle and thwarted many efforts by the English and French to colonize the island.

Juan de Cosa did not truly colonize St. Lucia. That accolade goes to François Le Clerc, a pirate called Jambe de Bois due to his wooden limb. In the 1550s, Peg-Leg Le Clerc attacked Spanish ships from Pigeon Island, now a National Landmark with historic structures and museums to enchant visitors.

St. Lucia and Colonialism

During the 17th century, St. Lucia became a target of colonization attempts by the French, English, and Dutch, each aiming to establish it as their own territory. The Dutch tried to construct Vieux Fort in the 1600s but were driven out by the Caribs. In 1639, the British dispatched 400 settlers to the island, but the Caribs wiped them off in less than two years.

In 1651, a French West India Company member acquired the territory from the Caribs to establish a French colony, and the English quickly sent 1,000 troops to retake the island. The conflict lasted until 1814 when the French lost St. Lucia to the English.

Let's go on to the present day. St. Lucia, one of the final European colonies to achieve sovereignty, officially declared its independence from the British Commonwealth in 1979. Today, it boasts a thriving and peaceful economy, underpinned by its autonomous government.

Modern St. Lucia Culture

St. Lucia's rich past makes it a melting pot of many cultures. Carib culture continues to greatly affect the island despite being combined with African traditions brought over during colonial times. English, French, and Dutch aspects merge with the rest of the island's culture, giving visitors to St. Lucia a distinct identity.

Visitors to St. Lucia may immerse themselves in the island's culture and learn about its history. Explore ancient Arawak archaeological sites or stroll through Vieux Fort's Old Town to get a sense of living in St. Lucia during the 17th and 18th centuries. St. Lucia's rich culture continues to reflect the island's heritage.

Geography and Climate

St. Lucia is one of many tiny landmasses that comprise the Windward Islands. Unlike the huge limestone areas of Florida, Cuba, the Yucatan Peninsula, and the Bahamas, tiny coral and sand islands, St. Lucia is a typical Windward Island volcanic rock formed over time. This territory was previously divided into regions. Lucia's physical attributes are outstanding.This island, spanning 616 square kilometers (238 square miles), is characterized by its elevated inland hills and dense forests. It is famously recognized for the distinct twin peaks of Gros Piton, located at 13° 48' 36" North latitude and 61° 04' 03" West longitude.

Petit Piton (13°49'59"N, 61°03'49"W) is a soft sandy beach on the southwest coast with a spectacular natural harbor. Mount Ghimier, the highest summit in the Central Range, is 958 meters (3,143 ft) above sea level. This disparity is also reflected in the quick shift in climate from coastal to interior places. The rugged landscape accentuates the many rivers that flow from central St. Lucia to the Caribbean Sea. Fertile ground for banana agriculture is spread around the island. Lucia has a tropical humid climate tempered by northeasterly trade breezes, resulting in nice weather throughout the year. The average yearly temperature ranges from 26 °C (78.8 °F) to 32 °C (89.6 °F) at sea level, but drops to 13 °C (55.4 °F) in mountain summits. Annual precipitation averages about 2,000 millimeters (78.7 inches), most falling between June and December. Hurricanes are the most extreme climatic change in the area and are known to wreak extensive damage. St. Lucia has often been spared major hurricane damage, but in 1980, Hurricane Allen decimated the agriculture sector, killing nine people. More recently, in 2010, Hurricane Thomas killed seven people and caused widespread agricultural damage, notably to the island's rapidly expanding cocoa sector. Crops.

Climate

Despite being in the tropical zone, St. Lucia has a mild climate owing to the impact of northeast trade winds. Because it is near the equator and the surrounding sea surface temperature fluctuates only about 3°C (25-28°C), coastal temperatures do not vary much between winter and summer. The period from December through June marks the dry season, while the wet season spans from June to November. Daytime temperatures typically hover around 30 degrees Celsius (86 degrees Fahrenheit), and nighttime temperatures average approximately 24 degrees Celsius (75.2 degrees Fahrenheit).The average annual precipitation varies from 1,300 mm (51.2 inches) at the coast to 3,810 mm (150 inches) in the highland jungle.

Culture and Traditions

St. Lucia's culture has developed due to the interactions between the many groups of people who have lived there throughout history. Each brought their own beliefs and customs, all reflected in the island's current existence. A visitor may find themselves driving on the left side, reminiscent of British roads, as they head to an Indian eatery located in a French village, all the while exchanging greetings in Creole patois with people they meet along the way.

One of the most apparent manifestations of St. Lucia's rich cultural past is its food. The island's lush, volcanic soil produces an abundance of food, and it is one of the main banana producers in the Caribbean, with six distinct types available. Lucia is not only rich in bananas but also boasts a plentiful variety of tropical fruits, including mangoes, papayas, pineapples, soursops, passionfruits, guavas, and coconuts. Local chefs blend the island's fresh vegetables with a diverse range of similarly fresh fish to make delectable curries, Creole-style meals, and pepperpot stews. Callaloo soup, created from a leafy green akin to spinach, is the national cuisine. The island's superb food has lately received worldwide acclaim, winning multiple gold medals in the region's most prominent culinary events.

However, St. Lucia's culture goes well beyond the table since the island has always been known for its intellectual and creative prowess. St. St. Lucia has been the birthplace of two distinguished Nobel laureates: Sir W. Arthur Lewis, awarded the Nobel Prize in Economics in 1979, and the renowned poet Derek Walcott, recipient of the Nobel Prize for Literature in 1992.

Understanding and enjoying St. Lucia's culture entails first learning about the numerous people who have contributed to it. The earliest were the Arawaks and Caribs, Amerindian peoples that lived across the Caribbean. They were adept hunters, farmers, fishers, and painters. Their principal crops were cassava, yams, and sweet potatoes, all of which are important to the island's cuisine. The coming of the Europeans devastated the Amerindians, and just a few St. Lucians can trace their ancestors back to this tribe. Farina and cassava bread, fish pots, and other indigenous crafts are among the rare remnants of Amerindian culture that have survived. Some communities continue to practice the old skill of fishing in dugout boats.

The second group to arrive on the island's coasts were Europeans, notably British and French. Though Europeans did not establish St. Lucia in huge numbers, they profoundly affected the island's history and culture. Even though the French lost the island in 1814, the British and French influences seem equally significant. The British added their language, educational system, and legal and political framework to the diverse cultural mosaic of St. Lucia. Music, dancing, and Creole patois, which coexist with English as the official language, are more visible manifestations of French culture.

At the same time that Europeans brought their cultures to St. Lucia, African culture was establishing itself with the entrance of slaves for European plantations and, subsequently, indentured workers. Their descendants make up most of the island's population, and their proud ancestry has significantly affected St. Lucia's identity as a country. African traditions have withstood the repressions of slavery and servitude to become the most powerful force in St. Lucian culture today.

Following the abolition of slavery, East Indians arrived in St. Lucia as indentured laborers. Most worked in the enormous sugar mills in the Cul-de-Sac, Roseau, and Mabouya valleys, as well as Vieux Fort, which still has a sizable East Indian population. In comparison to other immigrant groups, their numbers were insignificant. Although their original culture is practically extinct, the East Indians have had a significant and long-lasting impact on the island's superb food.

Chapter 2: Planning a Trip to St. Lucia

10 Travel Tips You Should Know Before You Go.

When travelers visit St. Lucia, they can be inspired by the island's natural beauty while participating in various exciting excursions. The island's lovely surroundings make it ideal for a romantic retreat with someone special. Of course, no matter how you spend time in St. Lucia, a successful vacation starts with adequate planning.

Plan Your Vacation's Itinerary

When preparing for your vacation, you should first decide what you want to do and see. Having a plan can enable you to accomplish more of what you want while also simplifying packing for your vacation. Although having a plan is usually a good idea, being adaptable and open to new experiences may enhance the enjoyment of any trip.

Make Copies of essential papers

If you lose essential papers, your ideal trip might soon become a nightmare. In an emergency, you should create clear photocopies of documents such as IDs, passports, and prepaid service receipts. Taking this easy step will save you a significant amount of time, money, and stress.

Notify Financial Organizations of Your Travel Plans

You must notify your bank, credit card company, and other financial organizations when traveling. This will prevent your accounts from being placed on pause. Failure to do so might result in a variety of problems. Most banks' apps provide easy, seamless methods for alerting them of your intentions.

Compare Rates and Prices

It's worth comparing travel and lodging options. Package offers might save you significant money, depending on what you're searching for. Remember that paying a little more for some conveniences, services, and benefits may be worthwhile. To compare pricing, click the "book now" option below and enter your desired trip dates.

Consider coming Off-Season

If your vacation schedule is flexible, coming to St. Lucia during the off-season may save you significant money. The off-season starts in May and runs until October. Even though it is off-season, plenty of exciting activities, events, and festivals are going on. This is when the island is most vibrant, and you're more likely to get a genuinely authentic St. Lucia experience!

Prepare a Packing List

Before packing, list everything you'll want and need for your vacation. Take some time to consider what objects you may bring to improve your intended activities. Before you go to the airport, verify with your airline about their luggage policies, weigh your bags, and double-check their size to avoid surprises.

Pack Efficiently

Bring as much stuff as you believe you'll need, but be sensible and avoid taking up precious space with products that can be found anywhere. Rolling your garments firmly rather than folding them can save you space and prevent deep wrinkles. Keep any important belongings, such as your ID, passport, documentation, money, credit cards, traveler's checks, contact information, and prescription, with you at all times, or store them in the hotel safe. Leave some place in your bag for keepsakes!

Learn Some Key Phrases

Most St. Lucians speak fluent English, particularly those under 40, but it's always a good idea to know a few words in the local tongue. Kwéyòl is mostly spoken in rural areas and small towns. However, certain phrases are popular across the island. Communicating properly is very beneficial, but learning some of the language can help you enjoy your vacation more by engaging in informal discussions.

Activate foreign Data on Your Phone

Most carriers now provide reasonable options for foreign travel. Many may charge as little as $10 per day to utilize your data while you are overseas. If your current carrier does not provide a package like this, local carriers FLOW and Digicel have inexpensive vacation deals.

Save Your Hotel Information

Another smart advice is to have your hotel's location, phone number, and room number on your phone. With everything going on, it's easy to overlook little details, even the most significant ones. This simple action may significantly reduce the difficulty of navigating new environments.

The best time to visit St. Lucia

If you want to enjoy the greatest weather in St. Lucia, visit between December and February. March, April, October, and November are wonderful if you want to avoid crowds but receive a bit more rain. You could also explore the three major cultural events that take place in May (Jazz Festival), July (Carnival), and August (Roots and Soul Fest).

For the ideal weather, visit St. Lucia between December and February.

If you want the greatest weather, visit St. Lucia during winter, when the temperature is mild and rainfall is limited.

In the cooler season, which spans December through February, temperatures usually fluctuate between 73°F (23°C) and 85°F (29°C), with an average near 79°F (26°C). Conversely, the summer season, encompassing June, July, and August, ushers in elevated temperatures, averaging around 82°F (31°C). This degree of heat may not be as agreeable for certain individuals.

December and February likewise have the lowest average rainfall, with around 5 inches each month, while October has more than 10 inches. What's fantastic is that rainstorms tend to come rapidly and intensely, but they don't significantly limit daylight hours.

Storms are also more violent over the highlands in the island's center.

The disadvantage is that these months are the most popular and costly visiting times.

Travel to St. Lucia from March to April to escape crowds.

If you want to escape crowds, visit St. Lucia during the shoulder seasons: March-April and October-November. These months usually provide great weather, with temperatures in the upper 70s or low 80s, but fewer people will be on the island.

The beautiful thing about St. Lucia is that the average temperature swings by just a few degrees throughout the year, so spending a hot day at the beach is never an issue, even during the shoulder seasons.

The October-November season is incredibly lovely, but it also has the greatest average temperature (82°F/31°C) and the most rainfall (8-10 inches each month).

Some vacationers may prefer the March-April season since the average temperature is much milder at 80°F (30°C) and substantially less precipitation (3-4 inches per month on average).

Does St. Lucia have a hurricane season?

Hurricanes are very unlikely to strike St. Lucia. Just 14 storms have been verified to have passed within 60 miles of the island during the previous 170 years.

St. Lucia is in the southern Caribbean basin, far from the so-called "hurricane belt" that affects the basin's northern region and the United States. Hurricanes also tend to intensify when approaching the United States from the west. This indicates that any storms that may impact St. Lucia will be quite minor in magnitude.

That being stated, the hurricane season normally lasts from June 1st to November 30th, with the biggest danger of a hurricane striking the island in August and September. If you want to travel during these months, we suggest getting travel insurance to be safe.

What is St. Lucia's rainy season like?

St. Lucia's rainy season extends from June to November, with an average monthly precipitation of 7-10 inches. If you don't mind a few raindrops, visiting during the rainy season might be an excellent way to save money on hotels and resorts.

In reality, many guests believe that St. Lucian hurricanes don't drastically impact the experience on the island. Storms can occur and may be fierce, but they happen swiftly.

Visitors like grabbing a bite to eat and getting out of the heat for an hour or two until the storm passes before returning to their beach lounge chairs.

Storms are also more likely to hit the island's interior; therefore, the perimeter beaches seldom get heavy rains.

When is the cheapest time to travel to St. Lucia?

The off-season, which runs from May to September, is often the least costly period to travel to St. Lucia. This is when hotel and resort prices are normally cheaper, and fewer tourists visit the island.

As previously said, St. Lucia's weather is relatively stable throughout the year, allowing deal-seekers to discover amazing off-season bargains while still having an outstanding experience.

When are the big cultural events in St. Lucia?

St. Lucia's main cultural events are Carnival in July, Jazz Fest in May, and Roots & Soul Fest in August. These are excellent periods to visit the island and learn about its culture firsthand.

What is the St. Lucia Carnival?

St. Lucia Carnival is an annual two-week event held in July. The celebration honors the island's African roots with music, parades, and costumes. It is often recognized as St. Lucia's most important event of the year.

You can attend a street procession before the event, followed by various parties and festivities around the island.

If you want to enjoy the finest of St. Lucia's culture, now is the time to come.

What is the St. Lucia Jazz Festival?

St. Lucia Jazz Fest is an annual jazz event held in May. The event showcases performances by some of the top jazz artists from across the globe. If you like jazz, now is the perfect time to visit St. Lucia.

What is the St. Lucia Roots and Soul Festival?

St. Lucia Roots & Soul Fest is an annual music event held in August. The event honors the island's African roots with reggae, soca, and calypso performances. It also serves to promote some of St. Lucia's incredible musical ability.

Packing Checklist

You've planned and booked your perfect holiday to St. Lucia! The next step is ensuring you have everything you'll need for your St. Lucia vacation. It's a laid-back Caribbean island, so casual clothing is ideal during the day, although many dress more formally at night. This section will assist you in creating your packing list for St. Lucia, ensuring you do not overlook any important goods!

St. Lucia Packing Essentials

Passport

Citizens of the United States must have a passport to enter St. Lucia. It must be current and more than six months from expiration.

Credit Cards

Credit cards are the simplest and safest method to pay for purchases while on vacation in St. Lucia. It takes up less space than cash, and cards may be canceled if stolen. If you're vacationing at an all-inclusive resort, your credit card may be enough to cover your expenses. Just be sure to phone your credit card provider and inform them that you are going.

Tip: Bring two cards and keep one in a secure location as an emergency backup. Also, note your credit card details and customer care contact information.

Cash

You should carry cash for taxis and locations that do not take credit cards, such as local markets. If you don't want to bring much cash on the journey, you can always acquire it from an ATM after you get to St. Lucia.

Most establishments in St. Lucia will take American dollars, particularly in tourist areas (though you may wind up paying somewhat more), or you may get some local cash. Remember that you do not want to carry a large amount of cash with you at all times.

Tip: If your aircraft ticket does not include a departure tax, you may need to pay it in cash at the airport, so be sure to inquire ahead of time.

Medicine

As with any vacation, be sure to carry all of your necessary medications. Put it in your carry-on bag to avoid losing your baggage. In addition to any prescription medication, carry some over-the-counter medications (such as aspirin, ibuprofen, stomach remedies, seasickness medicine, and antihistamines) so you have them on hand if needed. People tend to overeat when on vacation!

Keep any prescription pills in their original bottles to prevent problems.

Destination Information

When you arrive in St. Lucia, you may be requested to give the name and address of your accommodation, so have that information handy. This will also be useful if you're taking a cab to your accommodation.

Driver's License

Ensure you have a valid driver's license or a government-issued ID; financial institutions typically require two forms of identification. Additionally, possessing these documents is essential for renting a vehicle in St. Lucia.

Travel Insurance Information

Make sure you have your travel insurance on hand.

Tip: Photograph important documents like your passport, driver's license, and insurance cards, and save these images on your phone. Consider emailing these photos to yourself or someone you trust for emergencies.

Hand sanitizer

Nowadays, hand sanitizer is a must-have for travelers. Pack a few tiny bottles, and be sure you use them often.

Rain Gear

It is suggested to have a travel umbrella, poncho, or light rain jacket. St. Lucia's rainy season lasts from June to November. However, rain showers may occur at any time.

St. Lucia Beach Packing List

Beach Bag

When it's time to go to the beach, a beach bag is a convenient way to transport all your beach packing supplies. Check that it is constructed of water-resistant material.

Sunscreen

As with any beach trip, you will need lots of sunscreens. This is particularly true for a vacation to the Caribbean, which receives more sunshine since it is closer to the equator. Additionally, being on sand or water magnifies the sun's beams. The greater the SPF, the better while you're at the beach! While in St. Lucia, you should not wear anything less than SPF 30, although 50 or greater is ideal.

Bringing it from home guarantees you the required SPF and saves you money. I suggest packing some in your carry-on or personal item on the airline that is no more than 3.4 fluid ounces. In addition, you will need a lot more in your checked baggage.

Tip: If you're snorkeling or scuba diving, ensure your sunscreen is reef-safe.

Lip balm with SPF

Lips are especially sensitive to sunburn, so use a balm containing sun protection.

Sun Hats

Pack a wide-brimmed hat to shield yourself from the sun and avoid headaches, heat stroke, or sunburn on your face and neck. One that is crushable and fits conveniently into a compact bag is great for vacations.

Sunglasses

The sun in St. Lucia will be intense, so be careful to protect your eyes. Sunglasses are required, and they should provide UV protection.

Flip flops

Flip flops are ideal beach footwear. You don't want to take your costly shoes to the beach or wander about your resort. I normally pack two pairs: a fancier pair for dinner and another for anything else.

Swimsuits

You will most likely spend most of your trip in St. Lucia wearing a bikini. Ensure you carry various options so you don't have to wear a wetsuit.

If you intend to perform any water activities, ladies may wear anything other than a bikini bottom. Either carry some shorts to wear over your swimsuit or look for women's beach shorts.

Rash Guard

A rash guard will be handy if you intend to participate in any water activities. It may also keep you safe from the sun.

Clothing Packing List for St. Lucia

Shirts

When preparing for your vacation to St. Lucia, focus on selecting clothing appropriate for warm temperatures. Men should consider packing t-shirts, polo shirts, and short-sleeved button-up shirts. Women, on the other hand, might want to bring along t-shirts, tank tops, and light blouses. Additionally, if golfing is on your agenda, remember to include suitable attire for the activity.

Dresses and skirts

You'll want to bring a couple of casual dresses or sundresses and a skirt and top, particularly if you're staying at an all-inclusive resort that requires "resort casual" attire in some areas. Pack a fancier dress and matching shoes if you're going to a more formal restaurant. (Remember to bring a suitable purse!)

Cover-ups

Instead of changing into and out of your swimsuit, just put on a gorgeous cover-up. These are simple to bring and will save time preparing for supper or beverages by the pool. It is important to note that in St. Lucia, wearing a cover-up in public is customary.

Shorts

St. Lucia has a warm temperature; thus, both men and women should wear shorts. Cotton shorts, khaki shorts, and even gym shorts may all be worn throughout the daytime. Just make sure they are comfy. Breathable textiles, such as linen, are great.

Pants

For males, carry lightweight pants such as linen or khakis. Women may pack Capri pants or light slacks. If you intend on golfing, be sure to dress appropriately.

Shoes

The sort of shoes you pack will be determined by the activities you want to perform while in St. Lucia. It's advisable to include water shoes, flip-flops, and sandals in your packing list. If you anticipate walking extensively or engaging in sports, it's also a good idea to consider bringing tennis shoes.

If you wish to trek through The Pitons, pack some hiking shoes. Pack a pair to fit in if you want to go to a fancy restaurant. Also, if you're going to golf, carry proper shoes.

Underwear and pajamas.

Pack extra pairs of underpants for your trip and bring anything you want to sleep in.

Scarf, shawl, or lightweight jacket.

Women may wish to carry a scarf, shawl, or light jacket if they get cold in air-conditioned environments. In St. Lucia, it may become chilly after a rainstorm.

Tip: Wearing or carrying any kind of camouflage or military-style pattern is forbidden in St. Lucia, so do not bring anything with it.

Other Items to Consider

Camera

The amazing thing about today's cell phones is their excellent cameras. There's no need to bring an additional camera unless you want better images than your phone can deliver. If you bring a camera, remember to include spare batteries, memory cards, and the charger if it has one.

GoPro Camera

The only camera we suggest is a GoPro. That way, you may record movies of your underwater excursions or other locations where you don't want to bring your phone.

Waterproof Phone Case

When you're on a beach trip, having a waterproof phone cover might come in handy!

Phone Charger

You can't use your phone until it's charged!

Travel Adapter/Plug

If you're unable to connect your charger, you won't be able to charge your phone. In St. Lucia, the electrical voltage ranges from 220-240V. Therefore, it's essential to have a universal travel adapter plug and a step-down voltage converter for your devices.

Hairdryer

Most resorts now include hairdryers in the rooms but double-check in case you need to bring your own. (Again, bringing your own will not work on the outlets in St. Lucia, so pack an adaptor plug.)

Mosquito repellent and insect bite relief cream.

St. Lucia has a tropical environment; hence, there are mosquitos. Nobody likes to suffer from uncomfortable mosquito bites, so bring some mosquito repellent and insect bite treatment ointment.

Rucksacks or backpacks

You'll sometimes want to have both hands free, so carry a backpack for all your aquatic activities. It's also ideal for sightseeing or trekking if you intend to do so.

Beach Towels

Resorts provide beach towels; however, if you are not staying at a resort, bring a pair of towels.

Snorkeling Gear and/or Goggles

While all-inclusive resorts often include free snorkeling equipment, and you can always rent it if necessary, you may want to bring your own. Goggles are extremely simple to pack; if you use prescription goggles, you should include them.

Waterproof bags.

Waterproof bags are ideal for protecting your belongings from sand and water. You can bring these items with you while snorkeling or scuba diving, comfortably leaving the bag on the boat, assured that your possessions will remain dry. Additionally, they are perfect for trips to the beach or pool.

First Aid Kit

While most resorts will have a first-aid kit available, coming prepared is always a good idea. A compact first-aid kit should contain bandages, antiseptic wipes, antibiotic ointment, and pain relievers.

Luggage Tags

Make sure your name and address are on all your bags with tags. That way, if your baggage is missing, it will be easy to locate and return.

Tip: Use brightly colored luggage tags or attach a colorful ribbon to your bags to make them stand out on the baggage carousel at the airport.

St. Lucia Packing Tips

As you plan for your vacation, here are some pointers to ensure you pack all you need.

- Review your resort's dress code. Most resorts in St. Lucia are pretty casual, although they may feature one or two fancier restaurants where you may need to dress up a little.
- Pack a change of clothing in your carry-on luggage. If your checked luggage is misplaced, you'll have at least one new outfit. Because most of your clothing is lightweight and you will likely wear a swimming suit, you can fly with a carry-on.
- Do not pack valuables in checked baggage. Luggage is often misplaced (or rummaged through); although clothing may be readily replaced, jewels and cash cannot. The same applies to your prescription drugs. Many travel without bringing important jewelry, such as wedding bands, and wear less costly substitutes.
- Pack lightly. Not only will this simplify packing and unpacking, but you'll also be grateful while you're lugging your luggage.

- ❖ Leave some space for shopping. St. Lucia's local marketplaces sell some gorgeous products. You should allow enough space in your bag to bring home a few goodies.

The most essential thing to remember while packing for St. Lucia is to bring everything, you'll need to have a fantastic time! With these packing recommendations, you'll be able to enjoy your vacation without worry.

Budgeting Tips

As you plan your ideal holiday to St. Lucia, remember to balance seeing all this Caribbean paradise offers and remaining within your budget. This chapter will give you some great budgeting advice and tactics to help you make the most of your St. Lucia vacation without breaking the bank.

Set a realistic budget.

Before starting your St. Lucia journey, have a clear and reasonable budget. Consider your trip costs, lodging, activities, and everyday expenditures. Research the cost of life on the island, including meals and transportation, to ensure your budget matches your expectations.

Choose your accommodations wisely.

St. Lucia's accommodations range from luxurious resorts to low-cost guesthouses and vacation rentals. Consider your budget and priorities when deciding where to stay. You can save money by staying in modest accommodations while enjoying the island's natural beauty and attractions.

Plan and book ahead.

Planning ahead of time can result in significant cost savings. Book your flights and accommodations well to get the best deals and availability. To save the most money, look for package deals that include flights and accommodations.

Explore Local Dining

While dining at upscale restaurants is appealing, don't overlook the local cuisine. St. Lucia's local restaurants and street food stalls serve various delicious Creole and Caribbean dishes at lower prices. Local cuisine can be both delicious and affordable.

Use public transportation.

Renting a car in St. Lucia can be expensive, with additional fees for gas and parking. To get around the island on a budget, use public transportation such as buses or shared taxis. It's also a great way to meet locals and immerse yourself in their culture.

Take advantage of free and low-cost activities.

St. Lucia offers an array of natural attractions and activities that won't strain your budget. Hike the Pitons, explore the lush rainforests, or unwind on the island's beautiful beaches—these activities are reasonably priced and allow you to appreciate the island's natural beauty.

Limit Alcohol and Entertainment Expenses

Alcoholic beverages and entertainment can quickly add up. Enjoy local beers and cocktails at happy hours, or buy drinks from local shops. Look for free or low-cost entertainment options like live music at beachfront bars or cultural events.

Shop Smart

If you want to bring home souvenirs, shop wisely. Look for local markets and artisans where you can find unique and reasonably priced items. Avoid buying souvenirs in tourist-heavy areas, where prices tend to be higher.

Stay Informed About Exchange Rates and Fees

Be aware of exchange rates and currency conversion fees when using your credit or debit cards. Some cards offer favorable exchange rates and no foreign transaction fees, saving you money.

Keep an Eye on Special Offers and Discounts

Before your trip, research and subscribe to newsletters from local attractions, tour operators, and restaurants. Often, they offer promotions and discounts to those on their mailing lists.

A trip to St. Lucia doesn't have to be a financial burden. With careful planning and these budgeting tips, you can enjoy all the beauty and experiences this Caribbean paradise offers while keeping your expenses in check. You'll create unforgettable memories without breaking the bank by setting a realistic budget, making savvy choices, and exploring local culture and cuisine. Now, let's move forward with your budget-friendly St. Lucia adventure!

Chapter 3: Getting There and Around.

How to Get to St. Lucia

Getting to the stunning island of St. Lucia is an exciting part of your travel adventure. This chapter will guide you through various transportation options, including flights, cruises, and ferries, to help you plan your journey to this Caribbean paradise.

By Air

Hewanorra International Airport (UVF)

Hewanorra International Airport, located near Vieux Fort in the southern part of St. Lucia, is the island's primary international gateway. Here's how to reach St. Lucia by air:

- International Flights: You can book direct international flights to Hewanorra International Airport (UVF) from major cities in North America, Europe, and other Caribbean destinations. Airlines like American Airlines, Delta, British Airways, and Air Canada operate regular services to St. Lucia.

- Connecting Flights: If there are no direct flights from your location, you can opt for connecting flights via major Caribbean hubs like Barbados, Puerto Rico, or Trinidad and Tobago.
- Domestic Flights: If you're already in the Caribbean region, consider taking a domestic flight from neighboring islands to St. Lucia's George F.L. Charles Airport (SLU) in Castries, the capital city.

George F.L. Charles Airport (SLU)

While not as commonly used as UVF for international flights, George F.L. Charles Airport (SLU) in Castries offers a convenient alternative for those staying in the island's northern part.

By Sea

Cruise Ships

St. Lucia is a popular port of call for cruise ships, making it an accessible option for travelers seeking a Caribbean cruise experience. Major cruise lines like Royal Caribbean, Carnival Cruise Line, and Norwegian Cruise Line frequently include St. Lucia on their itineraries. Cruise passengers disembark at the bustling Castries Harbor, where they can explore the island's attractions.

Ferry Services

Consider taking a ferry to St. Lucia from nearby islands for a more adventurous approach. Ferry services operate between St. Lucia and destinations such as Martinique and St. Vincent. While this option may take longer than flying, it offers a unique and scenic way to reach the island.

Entry Requirements

Before you embark on your journey to St. Lucia, it's essential to be aware of the entry requirements:

- Passport: Most travelers need a valid passport to enter St. Lucia. Ensure your passport has at least six months of validity beyond your planned departure date.
- Visa: Visa requirements vary depending on your nationality and the duration of your stay. Check with the nearest St. Lucian embassy or consulate, or visit the official St. Lucia government website for up-to-date visa information.
- Vaccinations: St. Lucia may require certain vaccinations, especially if you are traveling from a region with health concerns. Check the latest health advisories and vaccination requirements before your trip.

Getting to St. Lucia is an exciting part of your journey, whether arriving by air, cruise ship, or ferry. By choosing the most convenient transportation option based on your location and preferences, you'll soon find yourself in this Caribbean paradise, ready to explore the island's natural beauty, culture, and adventures that await. Remember the entry requirements, and ensure you have all the necessary documents for a smooth and enjoyable trip to St. Lucia.

How To Get Around

The best way to get around St. Lucia is by car or minibus, though taxis are also available, water taxis around the island are plentiful. Rental cars can be obtained at the Hewanorra International Airport (UVF) in the southern town of Vieux Fort, about 35 miles south of Castries. Rates average about $70 a day.

Car

You'll need a temporary driving license for rental cars, which can be obtained in advance or by showing a valid driver's license at the car rental agency, the airport, or the police station in Castries.

Remember to drive on the left side of the road. Car rental agencies are clustered at the airport and in Soufrière, Castries, Rodney Bay, and Gros Islet.

Minibusses

Privately run minibusses serve as the main ground transportation for much of the island, with routes forming a loop between the main towns. Buses run at varied times depending on the route, but most do not operate on Sundays. Fares range from about $1 to $3. Minibusses have a green number plate with an M prefix.

Taxis

Authorized taxis have a light blue number plate with a TX prefix. Before you hire a taxi, confirm the fare. Fares start at about $70 from the airport to Marigot Bay. You can also hire taxis for island tours, which can be convenient if you visit St. Lucia via a cruise.

Fred. Olsen Cruise Lines

Chapter 4: Accommodations.

Luxury Hotels

Sandals Halcyon Beach

• Low-rise architecture makes it accessible to the physically challenged

• Fully air-conditioned Caribbean cuisine restaurant on its 150-foot pier over the Caribbean Sea

• 169 rooms with true personal service and intimate experience

• Meandering Crystal Lagoon Pool - 540 feet

• Tableside service at the Beach Bistro

• "Stay at one, play at three" free shuttles to Sandals La Toc Golf Resort & Spa and Sandals Grande St. Lucian Spa & Beach Resort. Guests can access even more exquisite facilities, including 27 Five Star Global GourmetTM selections.

Address: Castries-Gros Islet Highway, Castries, St. Lucia GM910.

Phone: 009 1 844-815-0937.

Ladera Resort

Ladera Resort St. Lucia offers luxury, romance, adventure, wellness, an eco-friendly attitude, and Dasheene's culinary delights. Each luxury room, set on a lush volcanic ridge 1,000 feet above the Caribbean Sea, has its own private heated plunge pool and an "Open Wall" design, which means there is no fourth wall, providing stunning views of the Majestic Pitons and the deep blue Caribbean Sea. This tiny 37-suite hideaway is located on a UNESCO World Heritage Site and is ranked as one of the top five gorgeous resorts in the Caribbean. All Suites include roundtrip private car airport transfers, breakfast at Dasheene, and the unique Ladera Ridge Hike to the top of the Ladera Ridge, from where guests can almost touch Petit Piton.

Address: Rabot Estate, Soufriere LC09 101 St. Lucia

Phone: 009 1 844-424-0642

Windjammer Landing Villa Beach Resort.

Windjammer Landing Villa Beach Resort, nestled on a verdant hillside overlooking the azure Caribbean Sea, evokes the beauty and charm of a charming Mediterranean hamlet. The spacious villas are over 60 acres, with 6 swimming pools, 5 restaurants, 4 bars, a spa, a fitness center, a kids club, water sports activities, and nightly entertainment. The resort provides an exceptional Caribbean experience for couples, families, honeymooners, and groups.

Address: Labrelotte Bay Box 1504, Castries, St. Lucia.

Phone: 009 1-877-522-0722.

Price range: From $522.

Serenity at Coconut Bay

St. Lucia's best-rated all-inclusive, adults-only luxury suite resort is the perfect Caribbean haven for discriminating romantics. Suites are spacious indoor and outdoor sanctuaries (1200-1900 square feet) with private plunge pools with waterfalls, soaking tubs, glass-enclosed showers, bespoke four-poster mahogany king beds, discreet personal butler services, 24-hour room service, gourmet dining, and more! Our boutique resort, perfect for romantic getaways and honeymoons, combines 85 acres, one mile of beach, and facilities with sister property Coconut Bay Beach Resort & Spa, which has eight restaurants, seven bars, five pools, a waterpark, and an oceanfront spa.

Address: Eau Piquant, Vieux Fort St. Lucia

Phone: 009 1-877-252-0304.

Jade Mountain Resort

Rising magnificently above its 49-room sister resort Anse Chastanet, a 600-acre beachfront property, Jade Mountain is a feast of organic design that celebrates St Lucia's breathtaking natural splendor. The 29 premium suites are known as sanctuaries, and they include sweeping spaces with bedrooms, living areas, and an extravagant private infinity pool that merge to create spectacular platforms floating out into nature. With the fourth wall eliminated, Jade Mountain's sanctuaries are stage-like settings to enjoy the full beauty of St Lucia's Pitons World Heritage Site and the Caribbean Sea. Jade Mountain has established a new benchmark in the Caribbean for contemporary design, luxury living, and distinctive resort and guest service experiences.

Address: 100 Anse Chastanet Road, Soufriere, 83310 St. Lucia.

Phone: 009 1 855-915-0638

Rendezvous Steals Time

Set on two miles of pristine sand and surrounded by acres of lush tropical plants, it's easy to see why StolenTime by Rendezvous' motto is "It's about time you introduced your body to your mind." It's difficult to imagine a more enticing corner of the globe for people to escape. It's a world apart from the every day, a soothing island escape. From the extensive expanses of empty beaches to the lazy river pool that weaves its way through peaceful nooks and hidden hideaways, every part of this all-inclusive luxury resort is designed to provide adults with the space and time to be alone.

Address: Malabar Beach, Castries, St. Lucia.

Phone: 009 1 758-457-7900.

Sandals Regency La Toc

•Lofty "Sunset Bluff Millionaire Butler Villas with Private Pool Sanctuary" provide 180-degree vistas, rotating 46" plasma TVs, a private Whirlpool and Infinity Pool, and completely opened glass walls for serene bedroom views.

• The elevated location of "Sunset Bluff Honeymoon Oceanfront One Bedroom Villa Suites with Private Pool" provides stunning vistas and the sensation of a "Resort within a Resort." With 24-hour room service, this holiday is characterized by exceptional luxury and privacy.

• A half-mile "Regal style Plantation" guarded entry lane leads gently down through the manicured fairways to an immense panorama and beachfront.

• Sandals La Toc Golf Course features nine holes situated immediately on the property and gratis green fees.

• "Stay at One, Play at Three" free shuttle exchange rights with Sandals Grande St. Lucian and Sandals Halcyon Beach property. Guests can access even more exquisite facilities, including 27 Five Star Global GourmetTM selections.

• Three stunning freshwater pools and four whirlpools.

Address: La Toc Road, Castries, St. Lucia

Phone: 009 1 888-726-3257

Budget-Friendly Options

Villa Beach Cottages

A small, boutique, beachfront hotel with premium, completely self-contained one- and two-bedroom villa suites located amid the coconut palms and beautiful tropical gardens of Choc Bay, giving panoramic views of the Caribbean Sea and comfortable, relaxed elegance with friendly, exceptional service.

Address: Choc Bay - Gros Islet Hwy, Castries, St. Lucia.

Phone: 009 1 758-450-2884

Price Range: From $260.

Ti Kaye Resort and Spa

Ti Kaye Resort & Spa, nestled on St. Lucia's tranquil West Coast, overlooks Anse Cochon Bay. With just 33 accommodations, two cafes and restaurants, the Kai Koko Spa, and a 600+ 'Wine Kave,' there is no finer spot for romantic leisure - mixed with some of the greatest snorkeling and diving on St. Lucia, right off the shore.

Address: Anse Cochon LC08 101, St. Lucia

Marigot Beach Club and Diving Resort

Marigot Beach Club and Dive Resort is the place to go if you want to unwind during your Caribbean vacation, and like St Lucia hotels and resorts with a laid-back and friendly ambiance that focuses on relaxation and enjoyment. Marigot Beach Club and Dive Resort is in a thick tropical jungle overlooking one of the world's most beautiful and fascinating bays. From the veranda of your studio or villa, you can see stunning St Lucian sunsets and just a few steps; you'll be on our palm-fringed white sand beach, drinking exotic drinks from Doolittles Restaurant and Bar.

Address: Marigot Bay 123, St. Lucia

Price Range: From $156.

Ocean View Hotel

If you're searching for a resort in Gros Islet, go no further than the Oceanview Hotel.

You'll like the peaceful rooms with air conditioning, and you'll be able to keep connected throughout your stay since Oceanview Hotel has complimentary internet.

The resort offers room service. Furthermore, Oceanview Hotel has a pool and an on-site restaurant, giving a welcome break from your hectic day. There is free parking for customers who bring their vehicles.

Travelers seeking filet mignon may visit Big Chef Steakhouse or La Terrasse. Otherwise, consider visiting an Italian restaurant like Il Pappa Trattoria Pizzeria Gelateria or Elena's Cafe Italiano and Pizzeria Italiana.

During your vacation, stop by Gros Islet Street Party (0.4 mi), a famous site within walking distance of the resort.

The crew at Oceanview Hotel is excited to serve you on your next stay.

Address: Massade PO Box 143, Gros Islet, St. Lucia.

Bed and breakfast.

Caille Blanc Villa and Hotel

The greatest kept secret in St. Lucia! Caille Blanc Villa & Hotel is this side of paradise. A private luxury boutique hotel with a 65-foot infinity pool overlooking the magnificent Pitons and Caribbean Sea. Each suite is distinctively furnished with canopied hand-carved four-poster beds, elegant private baths, and air conditioning with stunning views. Rent a single room for a romantic break with a candlelit supper, or book the complete villa property with all six suites for a beautiful wedding or family holiday. Our Pavilion restaurant delivers our classic breakfast daily, lunch, and entire supper options.

Address: Anse Chastnet Road, Soufriere, St. Lucia.

Phone: 009 1 877-748-6670

La Haut Resort

La Haut Resort is a three-star family-owned resort on a working plantation with refreshing sea breezes and breathtaking views of the Pitons, Caribbean Sea, and rain forest. La Haut Resort is perfect for couples, families, weddings, groups, nature enthusiasts, and health and wellness vacations. La Haut or Le Haut means "the height" in Patois, a French dialect used by St. Lucians. La Haut is located on a hill overlooking Soufriere, one of the oldest settlements in St. Lucia. The main Guest House, located on a 52-acre old coconut and cocoa farm, has a unique history. The main guesthouse, about 100 years old, was once a cocoa house for fermenting and drying hand-picked cocoa beans from the estate. In 1995, the building was transformed and renovated into a 6-room guesthouse.

Address: West Coast Road, Colombette, Soufriere LC09 101 St. Lucia

Phone: 009 1 758-459-7008.

Bay Garden Inn

Bay Gardens Inn is ideal for anyone looking for a tranquil, tropical vacation in St. Lucia. This charming hotel in the center of Rodney Bay Village is private and cheap, with a hidden garden location, cozy rooms, and a locally genuine feel for the perfect island getaway. Bay Gardens Inn, a highlight among St. Lucia resorts, greets visitors with exceptional service and contemporary facilities that make our hotel feel like home. Our central position lets visitors easily access Rodney Bay's gorgeous beaches and duty-free shopping, bars, and restaurants. All Bay Gardens Inn guests can access the Bay Gardens Beach Club on the prime beachfront of the four-star Bay Gardens Beach Resort & Spa, Reduit Beach. A free hourly shuttle service (5-minute drive) connects the Inn with the Beach Resort, providing access to sun loungers on the beach, unrestricted usage of Splash Island Water Park, unlimited non-motorized watersports, and complimentary Wi-Fi.

Address: Rodney Bay, 1890 St. Lucia

Villa Caribbean Dream

Villa Caribbean Dream is a wonderful alternative for visitors to Vieux Fort, providing a romantic setting and various useful facilities to make your stay more enjoyable. The four guest house rooms, which serve as your "home away from home," have a kitchenette and complimentary wifi for convenient access to the internet. The guest also has two one-bedroom apartments, the "Creole House" and the "Rainbow Apartment." Villa Caribbean Dream provides guests with patio chairs and a sun deck. In addition, Villa Caribbean Dream provides breakfast, enhancing your Vieux Fort experience. In addition, visitors may enjoy free parking. If you're searching for an excellent café while staying at Villa Caribbean Dream, consider The Reef Beach café or Island Breeze Beach Restaurant. Enjoy your time at Vieux Fort!

Address: Moule a Chique, Vieux Fort St. Lucia

Apartment Espoir

Apartment Espoir offers a unique experience, with 11 self-contained apartments (clean, bright, inviting Caribbean hues, well-equipped) and a wonderful view of the Caribbean Sea. There is a wonderful, freshly built wooden cottage with two bedrooms (colonial style) in the yard, adjacent to the pool. It is three minutes from the house to the palm-fringed sandy Labrelotte beach. We are the place to go for exceptional service, a warm and welcoming environment, English and German-speaking staff, wonderful excursions, and a home away from home. Don't simply dream it! Do it!

Address: 269 Labrolette Crescent East Winds/Marisule, Castries, St. Lucia.

Booking Tips

Choosing the proper hotel is important for arranging your vacation to St. Lucia. This chapter contains useful hotel booking recommendations to help you locate the ideal spot to stay on this wonderful Caribbean island.

Define your budget.

Set a budget before you begin your hotel search. St. Lucia has various housing alternatives, from luxury resorts to low-cost guesthouses. Knowing your budget beforehand can allow you to limit your options and prevent overpaying.

Choose the Right Location.

When choosing where to stay, consider your priorities. If you want to relax and unwind, look at hotels north of the island. If you want a more vibrant atmosphere with more food and entertainment choices, seek lodgings near Castries or Rodney Bay.

Research extensively.

Take your time researching hotels in St. Lucia extensively. Use reputable travel websites, check prior guest reviews, and browse the hotel's website for further information. Consider facilities, visitor reviews, and closeness to the beach.

Consider all-inclusive resorts.

St. Lucia has several all-inclusive resorts that provide extensive packages, including accommodations, food, beverages, and activities. If you like a hassle-free vacation with predictable costs, an all-inclusive resort might be a great option.

Timing is important.

Booking your accommodation at the appropriate moment might result in significant discounts. Look for special offers, seasonal discounts, and last-minute bargains. Consider going for lower prices during the island's off-peak season, which runs from June to November.

Check for package deals.

Some travel providers provide package offers that include flights and lodging. These bundles may result in considerable cost savings when compared to booking each component individually.

Loyalty Programs and Membership

If you have loyalty programs or travel reward credit cards, use them to reserve your accommodation. You may earn points or get discounts that may be used for your stay in St. Lucia.

Contact the hotel directly.

Call or email them personally once you've narrowed it down to a few hotels. Inquire about any discounts, hotel upgrades, or special requests that you may have. When contacting directly with hotel personnel, you may be able to negotiate cheaper prices.

Read the fine print.

Before finalizing your reservation, review the hotel's cancellation policy, extra fees, and other terms and conditions. Make sure you read the booking conditions to prevent any surprises later.

Secure your reservation.

Once you've decided, be sure to book your reservation immediately. Popular hotels in St. Lucia may fill up fast, particularly during busy tourist seasons, so book early to ensure your chosen accommodations.

Booking the correct hotel in St. Lucia is vital for a great and comfortable holiday. By setting your budget, completing extensive research, and considering location, facilities, and scheduling, you may choose the ideal hotel to stay that meets your needs and enriches your whole experience on this beautiful Caribbean island. Keep these hotel booking ideas in mind, and you'll be ready to make the most of your vacation to St. Lucia.

Chapter 5: Exploring St. Lucia

Must-See Attractions

St. Lucia, crowned by the Pitons' towering twin volcanic peaks, is the Caribbean's beauty queen. St. Lucia boasts a diverse range of attractions, encompassing crescent-shaped shorelines, quaint fishing villages, lush rainforests, vibrant coral reefs, cascading waterfalls, geothermal spots, and breathtaking highlands.

Castries, the capital city of the island and a popular cruise ship destination, displays a lively aspect of life in St. Lucia. Shop in its vibrant market and take photographs of its wonderful historical sites. Morne Fortune and Pigeon Island National Park teach visitors about the island's history, including the numerous conflicts between the French and English for control.

Adventurers will find enough to do in St. Lucia. Common activities on the island involve engaging in ziplining, scaling the Pitons, traversing the many clearly marked natural trails, partaking in horseback riding, enjoying sightseeing cruises, and venturing to explore the active volcano on the island. The western coast of St. Lucia offers exceptional opportunities for diving, featuring a rich variety of corals, sponges, and reef fish.

After all the excitement, you may unwind on St. Lucia's beautiful beaches with rustling palms or bathe in the island's curative hot springs. Read our list of the best attractions and things to do in St. Lucia for additional inspiration on where to go on this lovely island.

The Pitons

The Pitons, which are included in the UNESCO World Heritage-listed Pitons Management Area, represent the twin towering peaks and standout geographical characteristics of St. Lucia.

These remarkable peaks rise from the sea to high heights. The Gros Piton (big piton) to the south is 798 meters tall, while the Petit Piton (little piton) is 750 meters tall.

Both Pitons, formed by volcanic activity between 200,000 and 300,000 years ago, are considered tough to climb. If you're a diver, you may explore the underwater cliffs. However, most tourists admire them from a distance for their visual splendor.

Wondering where to get the greatest view of the Pitons in St. Lucia? The colorful coastal resort of Soufriere gives a panoramic picture of the twin peaks - notably from the Tet Paul Nature Trail.

Marigat Bay

Marigot Bay is undoubtedly the most picturesque bay in St. Lucia. It is best observed from a vantage point on the road connecting the major Caribbean coastal route to the bay proper. Lush foothills lead to the picturesque palm-fringed beach while yachts bob in the bay's azure seas.

The harbor is so deep and protected that the British fleet allegedly concealed from the French by covering their masts with palm leaves.

Marigot Bay was also the location for the 1967 film Doctor Doolittle, which has left an indelible impression on the names of various local businesses.

Hike the Tet Paul Nature Trail.

Looking for an escape from the heat, beach, and sea? Because of the island's unique geography, hiking in St. Lucia can be exceptionally enjoyable, and the Tet Paul Nature Trail near Soufrière provides some of the most beautiful vistas in southern St. Lucia.

This relatively easy to moderately challenging ascent meanders through the lush tropical woods within St. Lucia's designated World Heritage site, known as the Pitons Management Area. The hike usually requires approximately 45 minutes to finish. When the weather is clear, you can savor stunning vistas that stretch as far as Martinique and St. Vincent.

Along the peaceful walk, you may learn about medicinal plants and trees, taste rare tropical fruits, and see the traditional Amerindian cassava cultivation. You'll also notice lots of pineapples growing along the route. The ascent to the heavens, featuring its steep staircase ascending towards a breathtaking 360-degree vista of the encompassing scenery, stands as the primary point of interest.

It should be noted that hiking the path requires a nominal admission charge.

Soufrière

Majestic Pitons surround the colorful fishing town of Soufrière and wraps around a magnificent bay. This traditional St. Lucian town is approximately an hour's drive south of the city, Castries, and is an excellent base for a few days exploring the surrounding sites.

Soufriere was founded in 1745 and has a fascinating history. Its primary claim to fame is that Emperor Napoleon Bonaparte's wife, Josephine, was born here in 1763. The history of Soufriere is not without its grim chapters. During the French Revolution in 1780, a guillotine was erected in the town's central square. This site became a place of execution where numerous plantation owners and their family members met their end.

If you're going sightseeing, stop by the town center and visit the Church of the Assumption of the Blessed Virgin Mary, which has remarkable blue accents. Many colorful houses in town have filigreed balconies and tin roofs.

Other activities to see and do in Soufriere include hiking the breathtaking Tet Paul Nature Trail, visiting Sulphur Springs Park, and meandering through the Diamond Falls Botanical Garden. Relax on the beautiful palm-lined Anse Mamin beach if you prefer something more laid-back.

Soufriere is also the greatest base for challenging walks up the Pitons, such as the Gros Piton Nature Trail and the Petit Piton Trail.

The viewpoint on the main road to Vieux Fort offers a stunning view of Soufriere and its deep blue bay.

Morne Coubaril Historic Adventure Park

Morne Coubaril Historical Adventure Park, which overlooks Soufriere Bay, is a famous tourist destination. True to its name, this 18th-century estate combines history, culture, and adventure.

Cocoa, coconuts, and manioc are farmed here, and visitors may enjoy a tour of the operating plantation, tropical gardens, and model of a traditional hamlet. Guides illustrate how to process coconut for food goods and how to make sugar cane syrup, chocolate, coffee, and manioc. Following the tour, you may eat Creole cuisine at the plantation's restaurant.

Are you looking for something more adventurous? The most daring activity is ziplining with views of the Pitons, although plantation excursions on horseback are also offered. You may also ride horseback in the rainforest, to the volcano, or along a neighboring beach.

Location: beside Jalousie Entrance, Soufriere, St. Lucia

Sulphur Springs Park Scenic Drive on Mount Soufriere.

Mount Soufriere (Sulphur Springs Park) is the Lesser Antilles' most active geothermal region, named for the sulfur originally mined there. A road runs along the edge of the 274-meter crater, allowing you to drive inside a volcano, which is one of the most interesting things to do in St. Lucia.

Though the last major volcanic eruption on St. Lucia happened around 40,000 years ago, this volcanic hole continues to emit sulfur into the atmosphere and heat pools of water above boiling.

Observation platforms provide views of bubbling ponds and hissing fumaroles. After seeing the park, you may relax in the nearby medicinal springs and have a mud bath. Make sure you wear an old swimwear.

Diamond Falls Botanical Garden, Waterfall, and Mineral Baths

The Diamond Falls area of the Soufrière Estate has three famous attractions: well-designed gardens, a stunning cascade colored by mineral deposits, and curative mineral hot spring baths created for King Louis the XVI of France's army.

The gardens were planted amid coconut, cocoa, mahogany, red cedar trees, and plants and tropical flowers from all over the globe, such as orchids, heliconias, hibiscus, and anthurium. You'll also discover instructive exhibits featuring local fruits and vegetables, including christophine, soursop, and dasheen.

You may also utilize the relaxing outdoor pools or private bathhouses for a modest cost.

This historic estate also has the Old Mill Restaurant, which serves a Caribbean buffet to visiting parties.

Pigeon Island National Park

Pigeon Island National Park, located across from Rodney Bay, is a significant historical site in St. Lucia. During the war for possession of St. Lucia, the British could watch the movements of French forces in Martinique via strategic lookouts on the island.

Today, a causeway links the island to the mainland, and you may climb to the viewing point for panoramic views of St. Lucia's northwest coast.

The island also has the remnants of military facilities used during French-English fights, an interpretive center outlining the island's rich history, a small café, and two white-sand beaches.

Rodney Bay

Rodney Bay is a popular tourist destination on the Gros Islet in northern St. Lucia. Beach fans may enjoy the man-made crescent-shaped beach, which houses several St. Lucia resorts, restaurants, and stores. After midnight, Rodney Bay Village becomes a popular nightlife destination.

This secluded cove, bounded on the north by Pigeon Island National Park and on the south by Labrelotte Point, is a favorite docking location. The Rodney Bay Marina is one of the finest equipped in the eastern Caribbean, with various water activities. The hills around the harbor are dotted with impressive residences, and the region also has St. Lucia's largest retail center.

Reduit Beach is one of St. Lucia's nicest beaches.

Morne Fortuné.

Between the years 1803 and 1844, the British undertook significant developments in Castries, the capital of St. Lucia, by converting it into a prominent naval port and constructing defensive structures on Morne Fortuné, the hill that provides a vantage point over the harbor. It was on this site that some of the most intense clashes between the French and the English took place.

Morne Fortuné, which means "Hill of Good Luck" in French, still provides breathtaking views of Castries and the port from its picturesque overlook. Walking up here to take photographs is one of the most popular free things to do in St. Lucia. On a clear day, one can see to Martinique. The ancient defenses remain; visitors may see a memorial, historic military structures, and cannons.

Government House, the official house of St. Lucia's Governor General, is located on the northern side of Morne Fortuné and is surrounded by magnificently planted private gardens.

Mamiku Gardens

This gorgeous park, located on the island's east coast between Mon Repos and Praslin, is divided into five tropical garden zones, each with its distinct theme. Among them is the medical herbal garden, where you can learn how African slaves found and shared their knowledge of the island's natural flora.

Birdwatchers will be especially pleased here, as many blooms attract endangered and unusual species. Commonly seen birds include the golden oriole, black finch, white-breasted thatcher, and various hummingbird species.

You may explore the grounds on your own or join one of the guided tours, which include choices for bird-watching, gardens, and the history of the historic plantation. The plantation trip includes a stroll to the shore, while the garden lover's tour offers additional information about the plants and their ecology. Orchids are among the garden's most popular blooms.

The property was previously a plantation in the early 18th century, and visitors can now view the gardens and archeological excavations and riches discovered. If you climb to the archeological dig site, you will be rewarded with breathtaking views of the coast and Praslin Bay.

Parts of the garden and amenities are wheelchair accessible, including a balcony overlooking the grounds.

Address: V39X+GCF, Mon Repos, St. Lucia.

Hidden Gems

While St. Lucia is famous for its renowned sights, such as the Pitons and stunning beaches, the island also has some lesser-known gems waiting to be found by daring visitors. These hidden jewels provide a unique and genuine look into the island's culture, ecology, and history. Here are eleven hidden beauties of St. Lucia:

Treetops Adventure Park

The Treetop Adventure Park, set in the beautiful Dennery Rainforest, provides an amazing experience for nature lovers and adrenaline seekers alike. Zip lines and suspension bridges will take you into the treetop canopy, providing panoramic jungle vistas. It's a unique opportunity to see St. Lucia's tropical splendor from a new angle.

Anse Mamin Beach

While adjacent to Anse Chastanet Beach, which receives more tourists, Anse Mamin Beach remains a hidden treasure. This quiet beach, accessible by a short nature hike or water taxi, provides peace and natural beauty. Snorkeling and sunbathing are popular pastimes, and the surrounding plantation ruins lend a historical element to the experience.

Des Cartiers' Rainforest Trail

Escape the crowd and visit the Des Cartiers Rainforest Trail in the island's southern region. This less-traveled track leads deep into the jungle, where you may immerse yourself in the lush greenery, see tropical wildlife, and even glimpse the rare St. Lucian parrot. It's a heaven for nature lovers.

Fond Doux Plantation and Resort

Fond Doux is more than simply a place to stay; it is a historic cocoa estate that showcases St. Lucia's rich past. Explore the well-preserved estate with cocoa farms, natural walks, and quaint colonial-era houses. You may also attend cocoa-making classes to learn about the chocolate-making process.

Diamond Botanical Gardens

While the Diamond Falls are a well-known site, the adjoining Botanical Gardens are generally overlooked. These magnificent gardens in Soufrière contain exotic vegetation, mineral springs, and tranquil strolling routes. The gardens provide a tranquil setting to relax and observe the island's floral richness.

Tet Paul Nature Trail

The Tet Paul Nature Trail near Soufrière offers panoramic views without crowds. This hidden treasure provides breathtaking views of the Pitons, volcanic spires, and the Caribbean Sea. The route is educational, with educated guides describing local plants and wildlife.

Zaka Art Cafe

Zaka Art Café, located in the center of Castries, is a hidden gem for art and coffee enthusiasts. This quaint café serves locally roasted coffee and delectable pastries and has a gallery showing the work of brilliant St. Lucian artists. It's the perfect place to unwind, have coffee, and immerse yourself in the island's creative culture.

Pigeon Island National Landmark.

While Pigeon Island is not fully concealed, its historical importance is sometimes overshadowed by its natural beauty. Explore the remnants of military forts, stop at the Museum of National History, and ascend to the peak for stunning vistas. It's a fantastic combination of nature and history.

Latille Waterfall

Escape the tourist hordes at the Latille Waterfall, a tranquil and lesser-known cascade in the Babonneau area. The waterfalls are accessible by a short stroll through the forest, making it a pleasant refuge for people seeking privacy and a refreshing plunge in pure waters.

Marigat Bay

While not completely secluded, Marigot Bay is sometimes eclipsed by more prominent tourist destinations. This lovely bay provides a serene environment for leisure and aquatic sports. You may hire a kayak or paddleboard or just have a beverage at one of the bay's waterfront bars while admiring the breathtaking scenery.

Exploring these hidden jewels in St. Lucia enables you to interact with the island's culture, wildlife, and history more profoundly. Whether you're looking for adventure, nature, or peace & quiet, these off-the-beaten-path sites provide a one-of-a-kind and memorable St. Lucian experience.

Exploring Rainforests and Waterfalls

St. Lucia's beautiful scenery extends beyond its pristine beaches and renowned Pitons. The island also has beautiful jungles overflowing with various flora and wildlife and a wealth of breathtaking waterfalls ready to be explored. In this detailed itinerary, we will take you through St. Lucia's rainforests and waterfalls, exposing the hidden beauty and natural marvels that await.

The Rainforests of St. Lucia

Enchanted greenery

St. Lucia's rainforests, largely on the island's western side, are lush, green havens teeming with exotic plant species. Towering trees, brilliant flowers, and crawling vines provide a magnificent setting in which nature flourishes in all its grandeur.

Anse Mamin & Anse Chastanet

Begin your jungle experience at Anse Mamin and Anse Chastanet, near Soufrière. You may explore well-maintained hiking routes that weave through the jungle. Keep an eye out for the island's indigenous flora and wildlife, which includes the secretive St. Lucian parrot.

Edmund Forest Reserve

The Edmund Forest Reserve offers a more in-depth immersion into the rainforest. Guided excursions are provided to take you through this protected region, where you may see hidden waterfalls and lush foliage and potentially see animals like agoutis, tree boas, and numerous bird species.

Descartiers' Rainforest Trail

Less visited by visitors, the Descartes Rainforest Trail provides a peaceful retreat into nature. This hidden treasure is ideal for birdwatchers since it is a great place to see the St. Lucian parrot and other avian species. The trail's natural surroundings make it suitable for leisurely hikes and relaxation.

The Waterfalls of St. Lucia

Diamond Falls

Diamond Falls, one of the island's most well-known waterfalls, is in the Diamond Botanical Gardens near Soufrière. The mineral-rich waters fall in shades of yellow, green, and black, creating a visually appealing and relaxing experience.

Toraille Waterfall

Toraille Waterfall, located only a short drive from Soufrière, has a pleasant natural swimming pool at its foot. The rich greenery around the falls offers a peaceful atmosphere, and you may even swim in the calm waters under the tumbling flow.

Sault Falls

Sault Falls, hidden in the lovely town of Fond St. Jacques, is a lesser-known beauty. Its remote position provides a calm and private experience. A short stroll leads to the falls, where you can swim in the clear pool or enjoy the natural splendor.

Piton Falls

Exploring the Piton Falls near the renowned Pitons provides a unique experience. These falls, which can be reached by boat or a strenuous climb, provide breathtaking vistas and the chance to swim in crystal-clear waters against the background of the renowned Pitons.

Tips for Exploring Rain Forests and Waterfalls

- Wear sturdy hiking shoes with adequate traction.
- Wear lightweight, moisture-wicking gear for trekking in tropical climates.
- Provide insect repellant and sunscreen to protect against sun and mosquitoes.
- Hire a local guide for a more educational and enjoyable experience.
- Keep hydrated by bringing a refillable water bottle.
- Respect the environment by avoiding trash and following established trails.

Exploring St. Lucia's jungles and waterfalls immerses you in the island's natural splendor and diverse wildlife. Whether you're looking for a tough climb, a refreshing swim, or a peaceful retreat into nature, St. Lucia's rainforests and waterfalls have something spectacular to offer every visitor. So, lace on your hiking boots and explore the heart of this Caribbean paradise.

Bird Watching in St. Lucia

When you think about animal encounters in St. Lucia, you probably think of the unique undersea life that flourishes in the reefs and waterways around the island; nevertheless, the nation is also one of the greenest in the Caribbean, with lush woods and wetlands teeming with winged beauty. There are over 170 species present here, including at least six endemics, one of which is the St. Lucia parrot, which was saved from extinction in the 1980s thanks to island-wide campaigns and a breeding strategy.

Located in the Windward Islands, between the colder climates of North and South America, this little island country attracts birds from both continents, with North American species visiting from October to March and South American migrants arriving from May to September. St. Lucia's small size makes moving about easy, so you may see the country's many landscapes and identify an astounding number of bird species in only a few days. Read on to learn more about bird watching in St. Lucia.

Where to Go Bird Watching in St. Lucia

St. Lucia has a lot of birding locations, and the environments range from beaches to mountains to rainforests. However, you don't have to walk to the middle of nowhere to see colorful birds. Hummingbirds will gather nectar from the bushes wherever you stay, as will doves, finches, and pigeons flying about the grounds, while hawks, kestrels, and majestic frigate birds may be seen above.

Central Rainforest Belt

The Central Rainforest belt is a great place to see the St. Lucia parrot and other uncommon species. Your binoculars will take in the black finches, mockingbirds, and St. Lucia orioles, who regularly drop in at the feeding stations that border the lush walking pathways. The Soufriere Des Bott Trail ascends nearly 300 meters above sea level, with many opportunities to pause and enjoy breathtaking views of the Pitons to the north and the Soufriere Mountain range to the west.

Mamiku Botanical Garden and Estate

The Mamiku Botanical Gardens and Estate, bought in 1766 by Baron de Micoud, former governor of St Lucia, now includes over 200 plant kinds and is still a thriving banana and fruit plantation. It provides frequent bird viewing trips and is an excellent location to see hummingbirds, golden orioles, and the endangered white-breasted thrasher. It also includes 247 plant species, beautiful tropical orchids, ancient ruins and hiking routes.

Millet Bird Sanctuary and Nature Trail

This sanctuary, located around 10 kilometers inland from the West Coast highway, is home to more than 30 bird species, five of which are unique, including the St. Lucia parrot and the St. Lucia warbler. There are many educated forest rangers here to take you on a tour of the sanctuary, including a magnificent 3km circle hiking track through dense woods and open hilltops with a stunning view of the John Compton Dam, the biggest in the Eastern Caribbean.

Northeast Coast

St. Lucia's northeast coast is wild and scenic, with abundant wildlife, particularly aquatic birds. Grand Anse Beach, a calm stretch of white sand, is a popular nesting site for leatherback turtles, but it is also one of the few sites on the island where you can routinely observe nightjars, mask ducks, and, if you're fortunate, the house wren and the rare bridal quail dove. Other highlights include the beachside town of Gros Islet, where you can see royal, sandwich, and other terns; and Pigeon Island, which is connected to the mainland by a sandy causeway and is riddled with historic sites as well as brown, mask, and red-footed boobies roosting on a cliffside perch 300m above the ocean.

Quilesse Forest

The St. Lucia parrot inhabits the thick canopy of the Quilesse Forest Reserve. Several walking pathways weave through the area, passing by huge ferns, towering philodendrons, orchids, and anthuriums. These include the stunningly gorgeous Descartiers Trail, a 4km loop through seldom frequented territory that contains almost all of St. Lucia's endemics. Birding trips here are often coupled with visits to the Vieux Fort Wetlands, which attract a variety of shorebirds and waterfowl, including ducks, herons, sandpipers, plovers, egrets, rails, and more.

Chapter 6: Beaches and outdoor activities.

Best beaches in St. Lucia.

The greatest beaches in St. Lucia provide tropical escapes with white and gold sand, crashing waves, brilliant blue seas, sun, relaxation, and fun for everyone. The most frequent reason people visit the Caribbean is to enjoy the beaches, whether to play beach volleyball, surf in the waves, snorkel amid coral reefs, construct sandcastles, or just relax in the sun.

The beaches here are among the greatest in the Caribbean for beach parties, afternoon drinks, or a romantic stroll at dawn or sunset. Check out some of St. Lucia's top beaches to make your Caribbean vacation unforgettable.

Marigat Bay

Sit at the docks and watch the boats roll in.

Marigot Bay is a port community with long lengths of fine beaches and sparkling seas, gentle surf, and a romantic ambiance that has been portrayed in several films. Outstanding restaurants and modern, informal beach bars are only feet away from practically every beach around the bay, where you may enjoy an afternoon drink or an evening party.

The bay's moderate surf makes it ideal for wading, and many people come here to watch sailboats bob up and down on the sea or to slip out in a kayak and enjoy the sailing experience for themselves. Marigot Bay can be found on the western shoreline of the island of St. Lucia.

La Toca Beach

Enjoy a tranquil, calm sanctuary only minutes from the city.

La Toc Beach, located just south of Castries, St. Lucia, provides a bright, tranquil refuge with gold beaches, deep blue seas, gentle surf, and swaying palm palms. This peaceful beach is seldom crowded and provides a nice retreat from the city's hustle and bustle while just a few minutes away from Castries' attractions and services.

Just a few minutes away, you may visit a historic fort and learn tales about the past while enjoying magnificent bay views. It's a great spot to reconnect with nature and refuel for future excursions.

Grande Anse Beach

Escape the hustle and bustle.

Grande Anse Beach is a remote, tranquil length of golden sand and waves on St. Lucia's northeastern coast, with unending spectacular, undisturbed natural beauty framed by coastal cliffs. You may lean back with your toes on the sand and listen to the breaking waves on the coast. Getting here takes a short stroll through the beautiful tree-lined countryside.

The surf here is rough and not suitable for swimming. It is, nevertheless, an excellent area for a picnic meal. It's also a popular nesting location for sea turtles; you could see some endangered leatherbacks there.

Reduit Beach

Take a romantic stroll along the coast.

Reduit Beach is one of the island's lengthier expanses of sand, allowing a romantic walk down the coast while the tranquil seas soak your feet. It is one of St. Lucia's most popular beaches; thus, it may become congested. Shops and restaurants line the beach, and there's a nearby water park for the entire family to enjoy.

Water activities, including windsurfing, water skiing, and snorkeling, are very popular here. This is a visitor-friendly beach that is popular due to the many facilities it provides. It is at the island's northern point.

Jalousie Beach

Capture a photograph of rainforest mountains.

Jalousie Beach, also known as Sugar Beach, is one of the Caribbean's best beaches, with smooth, white sand and brilliant turquoise seas perfect for snorkeling and diving. This beach is well-known for its picture possibilities, and it is surrounded by high mountains covered in thick rainforests and flanked with swaying palm palms.

Suppose you have a waterproof camera and love snorkeling or scuba diving. In that case, you may capture photographs of an infinite variety of colorful marine life in the 1,800-foot plunge at the base of the mountains. The beach is located south of the hamlet of Soufriere.

Anse des Sables Beach

Try your hand at kiteboarding.

Anse de Sables Beach is one of the island's most gorgeous beaches, with nearly a mile of fine white sand and warm, clear seas perfect for swimming and water sports. It's ideal for a lengthy stroll on the beach with your special someone, with almost a mile of beachfront to explore on the island's southeastern edge. Here, you may attempt kiteboarding and windsurfing or just swim and relax.

When you're done visiting the beach, you may explore many local and national parks, including islands accessible by a 20-minute ferry boat journey. You may explore routes dotted with tropical flowers and view intriguing local wildlife, such as the whiptail lizard.

Cas de Bas Beach

Party in a beach cottage where Amy Winehouse relaxed.

Cas en Bas Beach is a popular hangout for residents and tourists, including a simple café and beach club set against a rough backdrop. The beach on the northeast coast is popular with residents who go fishing in the waves and riding horses along the coastline. You may even hire a horse and ride it yourself.

Marjorie's beach club is well-known around the island and has hosted many celebrities, including the late singer Amy Winehouse. It has a relaxing party atmosphere, pleasant service, and excellent cuisine and beverages, making it ideal for unwinding after a day of excursions.

Anse Chastanet Beach.

Catch a snapshot of a remarkable, beautiful rock formation.

Anse Chastanet Beach is a black-sand cove beach just north of Soufriere that has a lengthy stretch of dark volcanic sand and tranquil seas perfect for swimming, boating, and photography. A well-known picturesque rock structure rises from the sea and will undoubtedly be a feature of social media feeds, as will the tropical highlands that serve as a background to the deep-blue ocean waves.

The beach is especially popular with divers and snorkelers because of the vibrant, live coral reef near offshore and the steep drop-off sea cliffs. To top it all off, several alternatives for tropical beverages and Caribbean BBQ are only a few feet away.

Water Sports and Adventure

With its beautiful beaches, crystal-clear seas, and lush scenery, St. Lucia provides many water sports and adventures for those seeking adrenaline-pumping activities or just a calm day by the sea. From engaging in scuba diving and snorkeling to enjoying sailing and windsurfing, this comprehensive book will introduce you to the incredible underwater experiences available in this Caribbcan haven.

Scuba diving and snorkeling

Scuba divers and snorkelers will find paradise in the underwater realm of St. Lucia. The balmy waters of the Caribbean Sea are inhabited by vibrant coral reefs, a wide range of marine species, and intriguing sunken vessels.

Anse Chastanet Reef.

Anse Chastanet Reef, one of the island's most recognized diving locations, is a colorful burst of marine variety. While exploring this underwater paradise, you may encounter reef fish, marine turtles, and maybe the rare nurse shark.

Superman's Flight

For experienced divers, Superman's Flight is an exciting drift dive around Petit Piton's base. Witness the stunning underwater topography with high cliffs and overhangs while being transported by the currents.

Anse Cochon

Anse Cochon is a superb place for both snorkelers and divers. Explore the coral gardens, tunnels, and arches, keeping a lookout for seahorses, frogfish, and other crustaceans.

Night diving

St. Lucia provides spectacular night dives for those looking for an unforgettable experience. Watch the reef come alive with nocturnal species such as octopuses, squid, and bioluminescent invertebrates.

Sailing and Boating

St. Lucia's calm and clean seas make it an ideal sailing and yachting destination. There are alternatives for every level of expertise, whether you want to go on a day cruise, hire a boat, or learn how to sail.

Piton Sunset Cruise

Sail down the coast of St. Lucia to see the magnificent Pitons drenched in the warm tones of the sunset light. Enjoy a romantic supper on board while toasting to the beauty of the Caribbean.

Bareboat Charter

Experienced sailors can charter their own yacht and cruise St. Lucia's coastline. Moor in secluded coves and hidden beaches for a private getaway.

Hobie Cat Sailing

Rent a Hobie Cat for an active sailing experience in Rodney Bay's calm waters. The Hobie Cat is simple to operate and an enjoyable way to explore the shoreline.

Windsurfing and kiteboarding

St. Lucia's trade winds provide ideal conditions for windsurfing and kiteboarding. Whether you are a beginner or an experienced rider, there are places on the island for you.

Cas de Bas Beach

Cas en Bas Beach is popular among windsurfers and kiteboarders. The persistent trade winds and the shallow coastal waters create an ideal setting for engaging in these aquatic activities.

Lessons and Rentals

If you're new to windsurfing or kiteboarding, several reputable water sports centers on the island provide lessons and equipment rentals to help you enjoy these exciting activities safely.

Deep Sea Fishing

St. Lucia's waters teem with game fish, making it an ideal destination for deep-sea fishing enthusiasts.

Marlin, sailfish, and Dorado

Going after big game fish like marlin, sailfish, and dorado will put your angling skills to the test. Charter a fishing boat and embark on an exciting adventure searching for these valuable catches.

Jet Skiing and Waterskiing

Jet skiing and waterskiing are popular activities along the island's coastline.

Rodney Bay

Rodney Bay is a popular destination for jet skiing and waterskiing. Rent equipment and glide through the bay's calm waters while admiring the breathtaking scenery.

Tips for Water Sports and Adventure

- ❖ Prioritize safety by following guidelines, using appropriate equipment, and listening to instructors/guides.
- ❖ Respect the environment: Avoid disturbing marine life and coral reefs, and refrain from touching or collecting coral.
- ❖ Certifications: Before scuba diving, ensure you are certified and have received any necessary refresher training.

• Be aware of weather conditions, especially during water activities. Sudden weather changes can jeopardize your safety.

St. Lucia's water sports and adventures provide an exciting and refreshing way to experience the beauty of this Caribbean paradise. Whether you're a seasoned water sports enthusiast or a beginner looking to try something new, the island's diverse offerings cater to all skill and adventure levels. Dive into the turquoise waters, catch the wind in your sails, and embark on unforgettable aquatic adventures in St. Lucia.

Hiking and Nature Trails

St. Lucia's dramatic landscapes, lush rainforests, and majestic mountains make it an ideal hiking destination for outdoor enthusiasts and nature lovers. Whether you're an experienced trekker looking for challenging trails or a casual hiker looking for scenic walks, this comprehensive guide will take you through St. Lucia's captivating hiking and natural trails.

The Piton Mountains

Gros Piton.

Hiking Gros Piton, one of St. Lucia's iconic twin peaks, is challenging and rewarding. The trail begins in Fond Gens Libre and leads through dense rainforest to the summit, where you can enjoy breathtaking views of the island and the Caribbean Sea. A local guide is required for this hike to ensure your safety and to provide insightful information about the flora and fauna along the way.

Petit Piton

While not as commonly hiked as Gros Piton, Petit Piton offers a more demanding climb and is reserved for experienced hikers. The trail winds through steep and rugged terrain, and the ascent can be challenging. However, reaching the summit rewards you with panoramic vistas and a profound sense of accomplishment.

Rainforest Trails

Edmund Forest Reserve

The Edmund Forest Reserve offers a network of well-maintained hiking trails in the south of the island. Explore the lush rainforest, listen to the chorus of bird songs, and discover the enchanting beauty of nature. Guided tours are available for those who wish to delve deeper into the reserve's secrets.

Descartiers' Rainforest Trail

This hidden gem in the Babonneau region offers a serene rainforest experience. The Descartiers Rainforest Trail is less frequented by tourists, making it a tranquil escape into nature. The well-marked path allows you to explore the rainforest at your own pace while enjoying the sights and sounds of the lush environment.

Coastal and Nature Walks

Tet Paul Nature Trail

Located near Soufrière, the Tet Paul Nature Trail is a moderate hike that offers spectacular views of the Pitons, the Caribbean Sea, and the surrounding countryside. The route is educational, with educated guides describing local plants and wildlife.

Millet Bird Sanctuary

Birdwatchers and nature enthusiasts will appreciate the Millet Bird Sanctuary. This serene location is a haven for birdwatching, with the opportunity to spot numerous avian species, including the St. Lucian parrot. The sanctuary offers well-maintained trails for exploration.

Tips for Hiking and Natural Trails

- Guided Tours: Consider hiring a local guide for a more enriching and safe hiking experience, especially for challenging trails like Gros Piton.
- Footwear: Wear comfortable, sturdy hiking shoes or boots with good traction.

- ❖ Hydration: Carry plenty of water and stay hydrated, particularly in the tropical climate.
- ❖ Sun Protection: Use sunscreen, wear a hat, and bring sunglasses to protect yourself from the sun's rays.
- ❖ Insect Repellent: Apply insect repellent to avoid bug bites, especially in rainforest areas.
- ❖ Pack Essentials: Carry essentials like a map, a first-aid kit, a flashlight, and a whistle for safety.

Exploring St. Lucia's hiking and natural trails is a captivating journey into the heart of this Caribbean gem. Whether you seek challenging ascents, peaceful rainforest walks, or coastal hikes with stunning vistas, St. Lucia offers diverse outdoor experiences. As you venture along these trails, you'll encounter the island's rich biodiversity and breathtaking landscapes and connect with the natural beauty of St. Lucia's charm. So, lace up your hiking boots, grab your walking stick, and explore St. Lucia's natural wonders.

Chapter 7, Food and Dining

St. Lucia Cuisine: Overview

St. Lucia, a stunning Caribbean Island famed for its lush scenery and colourful culture, provides a delicious gastronomic trip reflecting its rich history, numerous influences, and plentiful natural resources. St. Lucian cuisine is a vivid tapestry of tastes, combining local ingredients, spices, and traditional cooking methods to produce an exceptional eating experience.

Culinary influences

St. Lucia's food reflects its past, with influences from Africa, France, Britain, India, and the Caribbean. This combination of culinary traditions has resulted in a broad assortment of meals, each with its unique flavour.

African Heritage

African culinary Heritage may be seen in the abundance of root vegetables, plantains, and spices such as nutmeg and cinnamon. St. Lucian meals often include starchy mainstays such as yams, dasheen (taro root), and green figs (unripe bananas).

French influence

Sauces, such as the classic green fig and saltfish stew, are influenced by French cooking techniques. French-style pastries such as coconut turnovers and tarts are also popular.

British influence

British culinary traditions have led to the popularity of meat pies and fish & chips. The English-style afternoon tea is also a popular ritual on the island.

Indian Influence

The use of spices and curry-based meals demonstrates an Indian influence. Roti, a classic Indian flatbread, is often served with curried veggies or meat.

Caribbean flavors.

St. Lucian cuisine is similar to that of other Caribbean countries, emphasizing fish, rice, peas, and colorful, spicy flavors.

Popular Ingredients

St. Lucia's abundant land and tropical climate provide many fresh, locally sourced ingredients, the cornerstone of its cuisine.

Seafood

Given its seaside setting, seafood is a cornerstone of St. Lucian cuisine. Fresh catches like snapper, mahi-mahi, and lobster are often grilled, fried, or cooked in tasty sauces.

Fresh fruits.

The island contains tropical fruits such as mangoes, papayas, guavas, and breadfruit. These fruits may be eaten fresh or cooked into meals, drinks, and desserts.

Spices & herbs

The use of indigenous spices and herbs adds flavor to St. Lucian cuisine. Common flavors include thyme, parsley, scallions, garlic, and the island's unique seasoning combination, known as "green seasoning."

Root vegetables

Root vegetables like yams, sweet potatoes, and dasheen are common in many St. Lucian recipes. They are often boiled, roasted, or cooked in stews.

Coconuts

Coconuts are a flexible staple of St. Lucian cuisine. Coconut milk makes creamy sauces and soups, while shredded coconut adds texture and taste to many meals.

St. Lucian food is a delectable journey through history and culture. Whether you dine at a local restaurant, consume street cuisine, or have a formal dining experience, you'll discover the island's distinct flavors and customs. St. Lucia's culinary offerings reflect the island's warm hospitality and people's love of fine food and company, from colorful markets to lovely waterfront eateries. So, while you experience the beauty of St. Lucia, be sure to appreciate the pleasures of its great food.

Must-Try Dishes

St. Lucia's port offers breathtaking white sand beaches and beautiful jungle excursions. A Caribbean beauty with a distinct colonial heritage that attracts thousands of tourists each year. French, local, and African traditions have blended here to produce an interesting way of life and a spicy and tasty cuisine that includes unique St. Lucian delicacies you won't find anywhere else.

Of course, at a big cruise ship port, such as St. Lucia's, you will discover worldwide food, including Asian and North American-style delicacies, but it is also worthwhile to taste the local "creole" dishes. The fresh seafood of the Caribbean, the wealth of tropical fruits and vegetables on the island, and the blend of spices brought in from abroad all combine to produce a one-of-a-kind culinary experience that tops the list of things to do in St. Lucia.

Here are the top 10 must-try meals in St. Lucia.

Bouyon

Cooked in enormous pots and eaten at family gatherings and festivals, bouyon is a delectable soup produced from local ingredients that must be sampled by those who visit this lovely island. This substantial stew, made with sweet potato, pumpkin, or yam chunks and ham hocks or pig pieces, satisfies the stomach while warming the heart. When eating bouyon in St. Lucia, you can always request spicy sauce on the side since locals prefer to spice things up with scotch bonnets, one of the hottest peppers on the planet!

Lambi

Like many Caribbean islands, St. Lucia adores the mollusk known as conch, which gives a huge chunk of soft flesh that may be cooked in any number of ways. On the island, conch is eaten creole style, which means it is strongly spiced before pan-fried as a distinctive St. Lucia meal known as lambi. Most restaurants in tourist districts and along the seaside offer St. Lucia lambi, and although it may seem weird at first, people often line up for seconds.

Fresh Lobster

Local divers who risk the deep seas of St. Lucia's coves every morning are responsible for the fresh lobster served for lunch at the island's restaurants. With enormous meaty tails stuffed with flesh, these St. Lucia lobsters are a delicacy that can be served in several ways on the island, from steamed to sushi, and they usually get wonderful reviews.

Callaloo Soup

The African influence on St. Lucian cuisine is evident in dishes such as callaloo soup, a creamy coconut milk-based broth laden with spinach (callaloo), and vegetables such as okra, potatoes, and garlic. Other variations of this local staple around the island include callaloo soup, which contains conch, lobster, fish, and other fresh Caribbean seafood.

Accra

When you get off the cruise ship and into any port town in St. Lucia, you will undoubtedly find Accra, a local favorite, served on the street. Accra is a delicious afternoon snack made from salted codfish wrapped into a ball and generously seasoned before deep-fried. It pairs well with your favorite beverage. Even if you're simply shopping in St. Lucia, grab one of these delicious snacks!

Green figs with salted fish

When ordering St. Lucia's national dish, don't be startled if it arrives with green bananas rather than the figs you're accustomed to back home. Fig is just the native name for the island's major export food. Green figs and salt fish have been filling tummies for ages. Thcy are pretty good when the fish itself — generally cod but maybe many other local species — is completely seasoned before being dried and cured for preservation.

Breadfruit

Breadfruit is a typical St. Lucia delicacy that grows on a native tree and may grow to the size of a melon. It is served with a spicy sauce or occasionally plain mayonnaise. Breadfruit, both starchy and sweet, is also eaten with major courses and made into delicious small "breadfruit balls" blended with cheese and veggies before being fried.

Pepper Pots

Pepper pots are a broad term for chicken or lamb-based stews cooked from scratch using whatever leftovers or local ingredients are available in St. Lucia's family households. While pepper pots are mostly a home-style dish on the island, more restaurants are beginning to offer them. They are currently ubiquitous. As the name implies, pepper pots are frequently quite spicy – so be advised!

Banana Cake

Enjoy a piece of St. Lucia's famed banana cake when you have a sweet craving. Many tourists consider banana cake a slice of paradise on earth, thanks to its nuts, spices, and mashed fresh bananas.

Fry Bakes

No list of things to eat in St. Lucia would be complete without the delectable morning delight known as a "bake." Simply produced by deep frying some sweet dough into a pancake-style doughnut, fried bakes are local classics that will wow the entire family.

Restaurant Recommendation

Great restaurants in St. Lucia capitalize on the island's reputation as a foodie's paradise inside an actual paradise. The environment is unparalleled, whether you dine by the beach or sit amid the trees. The sounds of the Caribbean offer the ideal backdrop, from natural harmonies to the greatest local vocalists.

Most of the best restaurants provide Creole cuisine and fresh seafood, with a few foreign cuisines for those craving a flavor of home. Chefs from all over the Caribbean visit St Lucia to establish their restaurants, so you'll be spoiled for choice the whole trip. We've compiled a selection of our favorite, terrific eateries for you in St. Lucia.

Pink Plantation House

Enjoy lunch in a lovely tropical garden.

Pink Plantation House is a Creole restaurant in St. Lucia that overlooks Castries. The mansion and art gallery are well worth a visit for photographs. With the pink, wooden colonial home concealed in the grounds, you'll feel like you've traveled back in time.

The onsite restaurant, serving locally sourced Creole cuisine, is the major draw. The Pink House salad is particularly noteworthy, made with grilled salmon and saltfish. We suggest contacting ahead to get a space on the terrace for breakfast. You will be greeted with nice, delicate fragrances from the nearby plantation.

Location: Chef Harry Drive, Morne Fortune, Castries, St. Lucia.

Open: daily from 10 a.m. to 3 p.m.

Phone: +1 758-452-5422.

Naked Fisherman Restaurant

Dine at the beach.

Naked Fisherman Restaurant is a peaceful pub and grill below Cap Maison in St. Lucia. It is in a secluded cove with spectacular views of the Caribbean Sea. There is a decent mix of short appetizers, full-sized dishes, and BBQ platters (after 6 pm).

As you would expect, Naked Fisherman Restaurant specializes inin seafood, with fresh catches on the menu daily. The menu includes spiny lobster, snow crab, and yellowfin tuna served alongside traditional sides like caramelized plantains and a Caribbean salad. Every evening, regular DJs provide a distinct Caribbean atmosphere to the venue.

Location: Smugglers Cove Road, Gros Islet, St. Lucia.

Open: Friday from 9 a.m. to 5 p.m., Saturday through Thursday from 9 a.m. to 10

Phone: +1 758-457-8694.

Rabot Restaurant at Hotel Chocolat

Make your chocolate for presents and desserts.

Rabot Restaurant by Hotel Chocolat is located amid a beautiful, organic cocoa estate in St. Lucia. While cacao is used in every recipe, this does not imply that everything is sweet; this Caribbean ingredient often contributes a rich flavor to savory foods.

Freshly roasted cacao is marinated in steaks, nibs are used to decorate salads and sour cacao pulp adds flavor to drinks. You must sample the sweets, particularly Robot Restaurant's chocolate lava. Ask about the "Tree to Bar" experience, which includes a tour of the cacao trees, cacao picking, and making your chocolate bars.

Location: LC Soufriere, St. Lucia.

Open: daily from 7 a.m. to 9.30 p.m.

Rum Cave

Enjoy a Caribbean drink with a shared plate by the water.

The Rum Cave is a modest restaurant on the edge of Marigot Bay. You may eat inside in the air-conditioned room, but the nicest tables are by the ocean, where you can hear waves lapping on the decks. Moored boats light up at night, and live music creates a beautiful atmosphere.

The Rum Cave serves fusion cuisine, like conch Bolognese, and local specialties like St Lucian fish soup. Order the famous Chocolaté Fondu for a unique dessert.

Location: XX7G+QWV, St. Lucia.

Open: daily from 10 a.m. to 11 p.m.

Julietta's

Caribbean great food at reasonable prices.

Julietta's is positioned above Marigot Bay and offers breathtaking views of the Caribbean Sea. You may walk up the hill or call for a shuttle directly to the meal.

Julietta's serves a wide variety of island cuisine that is inexpensive and well-presented. The restaurant specializes in fresh-caught fish and salads. If you can make it for brunch, you'll enjoy international favorites such as shakshuka, fresh burrata, and a selection of French croquettes.

Location: Castries, St. Lucia

Open: Monday through Thursday and Saturday from 9 a.m. to 10 p.m. (closed Fridays and Sundays).

Phone: +1 758-458-3224.

Orlando's

Locally experience exquisite eating.

Orlando's is a modest farm-to-table restaurant located in downtown Soufrière. It takes pleasure in utilizing fresh products grown on local, sustainable farms. You'll be given a personalized experience, with the courteous proprietor willing to explain the procedures behind each dish.

The 5-course tasting menu is refreshed regularly and includes dishes produced with locally cultivated ingredients such as blackeye beans, fresh mangos, and sugarcane. The meal also includes rum pairings. Orlando focuses on offering you an experience rather than simply a meal.

Location: Bridge Street, St. Lucia

Open: Tuesday from 7.30 am to 10 am and 2 pm to 9 pm, Wednesday-Monday from 7.30 am to 10 am and noon to 9 pm.

Phone: +1 758-572-6613.

The Coal Pot

Traditional techniques combined with contemporary eating

The Coal Pot is a waterfront restaurant overlooking Vigie Marina in Castries, only a few minutes from the cruise liner dock. The Coal Pot, named after traditional Caribbean cooking techniques, mixes history with contemporary fine dining to provide some of the island's greatest seafood.

The menu is always changing to make the most use of the day's catch. Local specialties like calamari Creole and saltfish salad lie alongside pita pockets. The grill menu always has a variety of steak cuts.If you happen to be in St. Lucia during lobster season, it's a worthwhile experience. This dish is prepared using age-old methods that have been handed down through many generations.

Location: Seraphine Road, Castries 00124, St. Lucia.

Open: Monday from noon to 3 pm, from 5.30 pm to 7 pm, Tuesday through Saturday from noon to 3 pm, and from 6.30 to 9.30 pm (closed on Sundays).

Phone: +1 758-452-5566.

Treehouse in Anse Chastanet.

Take in spectacular views above the treetops.

The Treehouse at Anse Chastanet allows you to eat amid tropical trees due to its placement in a forest canopy. An extensive cuisine matches the restaurant's stunning backdrop with Caribbean-style grilled scallops, marlin, and fresh daily catches. There is also an Indian cuisine if you want to go international.

Breakfast is a highlight for the majority of guests. You may have a traditional American breakfast above the trees, with panoramic views enhanced by the morning wind. After that, stroll down to Anse Chastanet Beach to swim and snorkel.

Location: 1 Anse Chastanet Road, Soufriere, St. Lucia.

Open: Monday through Saturday from 10 a.m. to 9.30 p.m., Sunday from noon to 9 p.m.

Chapter 8: Shopping and Souvenirs.

Local Crafts and Art

Its indigenous crafts and art brilliantly represent St. Lucia's lively culture and rich history. From delicately handcrafted ceramics to colorful woven baskets, the island's artists create a diverse variety of unique products that highlight this Caribbean jewel's ingenuity and legacy. This book provides insight into the world of St. Lucian craftsmanship and creativity.

Pottery

St. Lucia has a rich history of pottery production, with artists crafting useful and ornamental pieces utilizing skills handed down through generations. Local clay is moulded into exquisitely created products like bowls, vases, and ornamental tiles, often embellished with elaborate patterns and brilliant colors. The pottery culture is especially vibrant in Choiseul, where you can tour studios and buy one-of-a-kind pieces.

Basketry

Basket weaving is another popular industry in St. Lucia, where trained artists use locally obtained materials such as bamboo, coconut palm leaves, and banana tree fibbers. The baskets come in various forms and sizes and function as useful and beautiful pieces.

When visiting local markets and artisan stores, watch for finely woven picnic baskets, market baskets, and elegant trays.

Paintings and Visual Art

St. Lucia's stunning surroundings and colorful culture have inspired several local artists. You'll discover a variety of paintings, sculptures, and visual art that depict the island's natural beauty and way of life. The vivid and expressive artwork often depicts tropical scenery, vibrant festivals, and the island's flora and animals. Galleries and art studios in Castries and Rodney Bay allow visitors to examine and buy these art pieces.

Textiles & Fabrics

Local artists in St. Lucia create various textiles and fabrics, including bright batik patterns and tie-dye designs. These fabrics create apparel, accessories, and home design items. Hand-dyed sarongs, scarves, and clothes are popular souvenirs for travelers who want to take a little of St. Lucia's culture and artistry home.

Woodcarving

Woodcarving is another ancient specialty in St. Lucia, with artists expertly cutting beautiful patterns and sculptures from native hardwoods such as mahogany and cedar. Wildlife, cultural symbols, and religious icons are often used themes. Hand-carved masks and sculptures make for memorable souvenirs that highlight the ability and ingenuity of local woodcarvers.

Local Markets and Souvenir Shops

Exploring local markets, such as Castries Market and Anse La Raye Seafood Friday, is a great opportunity to learn about St. Lucian goods and art. Many handcrafted things are available, including ceramics, baskets, jewelry, and paintings. Souvenir stores, galleries, and craft cooperatives across the island provide an opportunity to buy original St. Lucian items while supporting local craftsmen.

Craft Fairs and Festivals

Throughout the year, St. Lucia holds a variety of craft fairs and festivals, which allow craftsmen to display their work and connect with tourists. The La Marguerite Flower Festival and the Choiseul Arts and Craft Expo are just two events where you may immerse yourself in the island's thriving craft sector, meet craftsmen, and buy their works.

Supporting local artisans

When purchasing St. Lucian goods and art, try dealing directly with local craftsmen or cooperatives to guarantee that your money goes directly to the makers. This helps creative people make a living and teaches you about the cultural importance and workmanship behind each item.

St. Lucia's unique crafts and creativity provide insight into the island's cultural past and creative spirit. Whether you're seeking a one-of-a-kind souvenir, a meaningful present, or just to admire the skill of local craftsmen, there are several possibilities to discover and enjoy. Explore the lively world of St. Lucian crafts and art, and bring home a piece of the island's culture and ingenuity as a keepsake of your stay.

Shopping Districts and Malls

The greatest shopping locations in St Lucia vary from tiny, local, artisanal shops to multi-story malls with big brand names. Most independent boutiques would gladly assist you in finding personalized presents. You may even witness local artists and crafters make their items in certain regions.

St Lucia's lush plantations and picturesque bays are home to various boutiques, allowing you to browse while taking in the breathtaking views. And the greatest bit? Many of these sites are duty-free. Don't forget your passport to receive significant savings on high-end products.

Castries Central Market

Pick up some fresh food and local products.

The Castries Central Market has several arts and crafts boutiques, eateries, and hundreds of vendors offering fresh local vegetables. This ancient marketplace is vital to St Lucian life, and at over a century old, it's clear to understand why.

You will always be greeted with a cheerful environment. The famous clock tower façade makes it an ideal location for taking selfies. The arts and crafts market is a treasure trove of souvenirs and presents, and the fresh produce area is ideal for purchasing tropical fruits and vegetables. If you want to feel the true energy of the market, come on a Saturday morning when the residents shop.

Location: 55 John Compton Highway, Castries, St. Lucia.

Open: daily from 7 a.m. to 6 p.m. (closed on Sundays).

Phone: +1 758-460-5596.

Baywalk Mall

A duty-free facility on Rodney Bay Street.

Baywalk Mall is a sophisticated retail center that has approximately 50 companies. There is a surprising mix of foreign and local goods, including clothing, accessories, souvenirs, technology, and cosmetic items. There is also an artisanal supermarket to buy wine, cheese, and international foods.

When it's time to eat, Sakuragi offers sushi, Jade Terrace serves Chinese food, and Amici serves pizza. Elena's, a local staple, serves handmade Italian ice cream, ideal for cooling down after a few hours in the sun. Baywalk Mall is near Rodney Bay, one of St. Lucia's most popular vacation areas.

Location: Rodney Bay Strip, St. Lucia.

Open: daily from 9 a.m. to 6 p.m. (closed on Sundays).

Phone: +1 758-452-6666.

JQ Rodney Bay Mall

Buy souvenirs and holiday necessities.

JQ Rodney Bay Mall is one of St Lucia's original retail malls, with dozens of stores spread over three floors. On the first level, you'll find a variety of cafés and eateries, while the floors above provide just much everything you may need.

The mall is ideal for purchasing tiny items you could forget throughout your vacation. You may browse for comfy clothing or get a haircut at the on-site hairdresser. If you want to eat like at home, there is an international supermarket. You can also discover a variety of souvenirs and presents for loved ones back home. The nicest thing about JQ Rodney Bay Mall is that everything is duty-free, so ensure you carry your passport.

Location: Castries-Gros Islet Highway, Gros Islet, St. Lucia.

Open daily from 9 a.m. to 7 p.m. (closed on Sundays).

Phone: +1 758-458-0700.

Sea Island Cotton Shop

Fashion business specializing in traditional woven gowns.

Sea Island Cotton Shop is a duty-free clothes shop located in Baywalk Mall. It sells a variety of locally created beachwear, accessories, and souvenirs, as well as some name-brand apparel. If you're looking for lightweight but durable footwear, the shop carries an excellent assortment of REEF sandals.

Sea Island Cotton Shop is recognized for its duty-free status; thus, purchasing presents here is significantly cheaper than at the airport. You may find something for everyone at home, from locally crafted decorations to traditional beer mugs and fridge magnets. There is also spicy pepper sauce to make Caribbean dishes at home.

Location: Bay Walk Mall Rodney Bay, St. Lucia.

Open: Monday through Saturday from 9 a.m. to 8 p.m. and Sunday from 9 a.m. to 2

Phone: +1 758-458-4220.

Diamond International St. Lucia

Buy the finest diamonds for your loved ones.

Diamonds International St Lucia is a shop specializing in Caribbean jewels and watches. It may be found in Pointe Seraphine, a duty-free retail center outside Castries. It has been a notable St Lucian institution since 1988; therefore, you can expect high quality and service.

Diamonds International St Lucia offers fine jewelry from Crown of Light and Safi Kilima Tanzanite and their brand, DI Diamonds. The staff is courteous and competent, and they can assist you in selecting your chosen styles. The nicest part is the gifts that are included with certain orders.

Location: Castries, St. Lucia

Open: Monday through Friday from 10 a.m. to 4.30 p.m. (closed weekends).

Phone: +1 758-716-8532.

St Lucia Rum Shop

Stock up on St. Lucia's favorite drink.

St Lucia Rum Shop offers award-winning rums from throughout the Caribbean. The little business is located near Pointe Seraphine, just south of the George F. L. Charles Airport. Rum is the Caribbean's preferred drink, and this store offers more than you could ever sample in one visit.

Real rum fans should not pass up the chance to try some St Lucian delicacies like Bounty and Admiral Rodney. There are several variations available, including light, dark, gold, spicy, and everything in between. There's usually welcoming environment and experienced personnel are eager to suggest a rum that matches your preferences.

Location: Pointe Seraphine, Port Castries, St. Lucia.

Open: Monday-Friday and Sunday from 9 a.m. to 4.30 p.m.; Saturday from 9 a.m. to 2

Phone: +1 758-451-9040.

Caribelle Batik

Discover how traditional Caribbean clothing is manufactured.

Caribelle Batik is a St Lucia-based business that sells handwoven cotton textiles. The business is located in Castries, nestled deep inside the tropical grounds of the Howelton Estate. You may undertake various activities in the vicinity before or after shopping.

Caribelle Batik employs the best local cotton fabrics created in the basement workshop. You may watch the painters at work while buying your favorite Caribbean-inspired clothing. The estate also contains various workshops that produce local specialties like chocolate.

Location: Old Victoria Road Morne Fortune Castries, St. Lucia

Open: Monday through Saturday from 8 a.m. to 5 p.m. (closed on Sundays).

Phone: +1 758-452-3785.

Chapter 9: Nightlife and Entertainment.

St. Lucia, a tropical paradise known for its natural beauty, has a dynamic and active nightlife scene. The world of entertainment and nighttime escapades begins after the sun goes down on this Caribbean jewel. Whether you want a romantic evening beneath the stars, a wild party, or cultural events, St. Lucia's nightlife provides something for everyone.

Beach Bars

St. Lucia beach bars allow you to recline on limitless lengths of soft sand with a rainforest background and a perpetual party feel while sipping on a refreshing rum drink. Here, you'll discover outstanding rum punch and handmade cocktails, terrific beer, beautiful wines, and wonderful cuisine prepared by some of the greatest chefs in town.

Whether you're looking for wine, beer, fresh-caught seafood, or Caribbean BBQ, or simply want to dance and party the days and nights away, the pubs and clubs here will provide it. Check out some of St. Lucia's greatest beach clubs for morning coffee, bistro lunch, and late-night parties.

Bayside Bar, Sugar Beach.

Experience a love for Caribbean Heritage.

Bayside Bar at Sugar Beach fully uses its beach-meets-jungle settings, serving meals with a Caribbean flair and providing live entertainment with a casual ambiance. Craft pizza, specialty sandwiches, and grilled conch are available at this establishment. The menu options are extensive and diverse, with something for everyone, whether you're looking for lunch, supper, or late-night drinks. Not only is it tasty, but it also reflects the region's cultural past.

While casual wear is acceptable throughout the day, the bar and restaurant promote resort chic attire for dinner and night. So, grab a mojito with a twist and enjoy the beach on one side and the forest on the other.

Location: Val des Pitons Forbidden Beach La Baie de Silence Soufrière, St. Lucia

Open: daily from 12.30 p.m. to 3 p.m. and 6 p.m. to 10

Phone: +1 758-456-8000.

Marjorie's

Dine where Amy Winehouse sat!

Marjorie's Beach Bar at Cas en Bas Beach serves local handmade Caribbean-style food with specialty rum punch, loungers, and kite surfing in an iconic setting. This pub is said to have been a favorite stop for pop diva Amy Winehouse, and it still has a vibrant ambiance that locals and tourists enjoy. One of their menu highlights is their Caribbean jerk chicken.

You'll find plenty of entertainment here, from watching people ride horses down the beach to live music performances and breathtaking ocean vistas. There will be no glamor, glam, or flashing lights here. You'll receive a true Caribbean bar experience with fresh and excellent local cuisine.

Location: 33RF+C59, Gros Islet, St. Lucia.

Phone: +1 758-520-0001.

Spinnakers Beach Bar & Grill on Reduit Beach

Enjoy basic, uncomplicated meals with stunning views.

Spinnakers Beach Bar & Grill on Reduit Beach provides a basic, uncomplicated experience with breathtaking views and everyday happy hours with a vibrant ambiance. They're well-known for their martinis and house drinks, such as the Piton Snow, which combines crushed ice, lime juice, coconut cream, and rum. It's a lively venue with pleasant personnel and customers that range from beachgoers to cruise ship passengers to yachters enjoying the open sea.

It is also well-known among beachgoers as a good spot to start the day. They open for breakfast; nothing beats sipping coffee as the Caribbean wind blows over your hair.

Location: 32GW+G59, Gros Islet, St. Lucia.

Open: daily from 9 a.m. to 11 p.m.

Phone: +1 758-452-8491.

Roots Beach Bar, Marigot Bay.

Relax with peaceful Rastafarian vibes.

Roots Beach Bar on Marigot Bay is distinguished by a brilliantly painted wooden hut in Rastafarian red, yellow, and green that serves chilled beer and a peaceful atmosphere. The spicy chicken grilled over a charcoal barbecue is the specialty dish, towering palm trees providing shelter from the blazing Caribbean heat. You may sit at the bar and speak with the proprietors, who like meeting new people while recharging your batteries in a relaxed atmosphere.

Here, you may enjoy delicious beverages and snacks while listening to reggae music and watching the beautiful blue surf smash on the smooth beach. It's the quintessential Caribbean beach bar, providing a slice of paradise by the water.

Location: La Bas Beach, Marigot Bay, St. Lucia.

Phone: +1 758-719-9283.

Jambe de Bois, Pigeon Island.

Find a hidden gem food stand.

Jambe de Bois on Pigeon Island is a hidden treasure food stand in the center of a national park, providing seaside views, island vibes, and tasty basic cuisine. The food stand comprises stone and driftwood, a thatched roof, a deck with picnic tables, and a comfortable and informal atmosphere. Enjoy happy hour by sitting back with a beverage and eating salads, sandwiches, local curries, and seafood.

Every weekend, residents gather here to enjoy live jazz music. You may also go inside to see a wonderful art gallery with local works for sale, which make great souvenirs to take home.

Location: 32RP+P4 Gros Islet, St. Lucia.

SeaGrapes Beach Bar & Restaurant in Gros Islet

Discover the distinctive St. Lucian culinary tradition.

SeaGrapes Beach Bar & Restaurant on Gros Islet offers authentic St. Lucian cuisine from fresh seafood caught right from the boat, with a calm barefoot beach atmosphere. You can sit down and eat excellent cuisine matched with handmade drinks, all in a cove with beautiful views of Pigeon Island National Park. The dress code is casual, the staff and clientele are pleasant, and the surroundings are spotless.

SeaGrapes is open for lunch and supper, with late-night service twice weekly. It is part of the Bay Gardens Beach Resort and Spa, but it is accessible to the public, so swing by for an unforgettable dining experience.

Location: Rodney Bay, St. Lucia.

Open: Monday, Wednesday, and Saturday from 10 a.m. to 5 p.m.; Sunday and Tuesday from 10 a.m. to 10

Phone: +1 758-457-8531.

Nightclubs

Pulse nightclub

Address: Rodney Bay, Gros Islet.

Operating hours: Fridays and Saturdays from 10:00 PM to 4:00 AM.

Pulse Nightclub in Rodney Bay provides a lively environment with top DJs performing Caribbean and worldwide music. It's a favorite hangout for people eager to dance the night away in a boisterous party atmosphere.

Blue Monkey Bar

Address: 1161 Cacao Lane, Rodney Bay, Gros Islet.

Hours of operation: Wednesday-Sunday, 8:00 PM-2:00 AM.

Blue Monkey Bar offers a unique combination of music genres such as reggae, dancehall, and hip-hop. Its laid-back atmosphere is ideal for a casual night out with friends.

Kaiso Blues Cafe

Address: Upstairs at #2 Jeremy Street, Castries.

Operating hours: Fridays and Saturdays from 8:00 PM to 12:00 AM.

Kaiso Blues Café provides a unique nightlife experience, including live jazz, blues, and Caribbean music. Enjoy an elegant evening with music, beverages, and a warm environment.

Club Whispers

Address: La Place Carenage, Jeremie Street, Castries.

Opening hours: Thursdays to Saturdays, 9:00 PM to 3:00 AM.

Club Whispers is a hip venue in the center of Castries. It covers a variety of musical styles, including soca, reggae, and hip-hop. The club's modern decor and lively atmosphere make it a popular destination for a night of dancing and entertainment.

Sky Lounge

Address: Baywalk Mall in Rodney Bay, Gros Islet.

Opening hours: Thursdays to Saturdays from 8:00 PM to 2:00 AM.

The Sky Lounge at the Baywalk Mall provides a rooftop experience with breathtaking views over Rodney Bay. It's well-known for its drink menu, live DJs and a diverse selection of Caribbean and world music.

Delirious

Address: La Place Carenage, Jeremie Street, Castries.

Opening hours: Thursdays to Saturdays from 8:00 PM to 2:00 AM.

Delirius is a renowned nightlife establishment in Castries that plays various music, including reggae, dancehall, and soca. The club's dynamic atmosphere and outdoor seating make it popular among residents and tourists.

Wingz-N-Tingz

Address: Reduit Beach Avenue, Rodney Bay, Gros Islet.

Hours of operation: 10:00 AM to 3:00 AM on Wednesdays and Sundays.

Wingz-N-Tingz is a seaside pub and nightclub noted for its relaxed atmosphere during the day and exciting parties at night. Experience beverages, live music, and a beachfront environment.

Cultural Events and Festivals

With our guide to St Lucia's festivals, you may dance beneath the stars, eat Caribbean food, and enjoy the best island culture.

With a rich history and lively culture, this Caribbean island's festivals provide live music, wonderful street cuisine, and a party atmosphere. The events listed below take place throughout the year, making it simple to attend at least one during your trip to St Lucia.

We've compiled a list of the most anticipated events in St Lucia so you can begin arranging your vacation schedule.

St. Lucia Jazz Festival

When? May

Where: Multiple venues

The annual St. Lucia Jazz Festival fills the Caribbean island with the sounds of well-known performers performing saxophones, trumpets, and bass guitars.

Previous lineups have included R&B and jazz performer Ledisi, trumpeter Etienne Charles, and six-time Grammy-winning bassist Christian McBride.

The festival is presented in partnership with Jazz at Lincoln Center, a center for concerts, educational programs, and festivals, and runs over many days. It's held several places over the island, so you'll have many opportunities to dance to the music.

Fisherman's Feast (Fête Pêche)

When? June 28th.

Where: Across St. Lucia

On the final Sunday of June, St Lucia's fishermen commemorate this yearly holiday, similar to Thanksgiving in the United States.

This celebration is considered one of the most significant in the fishing calendar since it allows them to express gratitude for another year of wealth and spectacular catches. Expect delicious cuisine during community meals, villagers dressed in their finest attire to attend church services, and fishing boats blessed along the coast to commemorate this event.

St. Lucia's Carnival

When? June and July.

Where: Pigeon Point and other locations.

The annual St. Lucia Carnival, the island's most popular event, is a month-long celebration of color, culture, and innovation.

The carnival's jam-packed agenda includes J'ouvert street parties, boat rides, music, and other activities, culminating in a two-day parade. Live bands and DJs provide the soundtrack, while residents and costumed dancers sway to the music in honor of Caribbean culture.

Mercury Fest

When: summer.

Where: Pigeon Island Beach.

Mercury Fest hailed as one of the Caribbean's greatest beach parties, is a must-see summer event.

It's a party in paradise, with French-Caribbean visitors and hundreds of boats from Martinique, Guadalupe, St Vincent, Barbados, and Trinidad. Expect to dance to the greatest local and French DJs and other remarkable performers, sip on refreshing drinks, and enjoy the freshest cuisine.

Roots & Soul

When? August.

Where: Pigeon Island.

The three-day Roots & Soul event brings renowned reggae, R&B, hip-hop, and soul acts to St. Lucia.

The main stage is on Pigeon Island, and prior performances include UB40, Leee John, Mya, and Ginuwine.

Some live performances are free to view, while others demand a charge and must be reserved in advance.

Creole Heritage Month

When? October.

Where: Across St. Lucia

Discover St. Lucia's rich cultural, ethnic, and creative legacy during this month-long festival, which includes art, music, gastronomy, and more. Four cities or towns are selected each year to host the festivities, so watch for further information as the event approaches.

Throughout the month of celebrations, expect to see colorful madras fabric worn by residents and utilized in décor across the island, as well as storytelling dances and presentations in communal areas and genuine Creole cuisine in many resorts and restaurants.

The celebration finishes on the final Sunday of October with Jounen Kwéyòl, a day to honor the island's history. Try some typical St Lucian food and dance the night away during the procession.

It's an excellent chance to learn more about St. Lucia's history while having a good time.

St. Lucia's Food and Rum Festival

When? September.

Where: Across St. Lucia

The three-day St. Lucia Food and Run Festival celebrates the greatest of St. Lucia's culinary and rum history.

Several award-winning chefs make dishes inspired by the island's distinct cuisine, which combines flavors from French, British, African, and Indian cooking.

Wellness Music Festival

When? September.

Where: Pigeon Island.

Feed your mind, body, and soul at the Health Music Festival, which combines health with music!

Starting at the BodyHoliday, one of the world's finest wellness resorts, this ecologically aware festival will include a variety of holistic practitioners, nutritionists, yoga instructors, and others eager to offer their secrets to help you live a healthier life.

Music is an important aspect of this festival, and a variety of worldwide, regional, and local performers, all of whom advocate for a wellness-focused lifestyle, will take the stage.

Festival of Lights

When? December 13th.

Where: Across St. Lucia

This is a memorable holiday, with thousands gathering around St Lucia to celebrate light triumphing over darkness with a beautiful display of lanterns and fireworks. A stunning lantern competition is held in the first week of December, followed by a parade on the 12th, which serves as both a festive celebration and a Christmas entertainment.

Visitors to this event will remember being surrounded by spectacular lit-up displays, a vibrant environment, and the great St Lucian culture and Heritage being celebrated.

Chapter 10: Cultural Etiquette and Local Laws.

Understanding St. Lucia Etiquette.

Understanding and observing local etiquette while visiting St. Lucia, a Caribbean Island with a distinct culture, is critical to having a good and courteous trip. While St. Lucia has its customs and traditions, it is not Puerto Rico; yet, adhering to key etiquette guidelines can help you navigate social encounters effectively and enjoy the locals' warm welcome.

Dos and Don'ts for Visitors to St. Lucia.

Visiting St. Lucia, a beautiful Caribbean island with a rich cultural legacy, requires knowledge of local traditions and etiquette for a polite and pleasurable trip. Here are some dos and don'ts to remember during your stay:

Dos

Respect the local customs and traditions.

Participate in local festivals, events, and customs to celebrate the culture. St. Lucia boasts a bustling calendar of events that provide insight into the island's rich history.

Greet locals with courtesy.

- ❖ Locals like pleasant greetings. Use words such as "hello," "good morning," or "good afternoon" as needed.
- ❖ When addressing someone, use titles like "Mr." or "Mrs." followed by their last name to show respect, unless they want to be addressed by their first name.

Learn about the Creole language.

Kweyol, a Creole language based on French, is commonly spoken in St. Lucia. Learning basic languages will help you connect with the locals while respecting their culture.

Punctuality

Although St. Lucia works on "island time," it's crucial to be on time for appointments, excursions, and reservations. Respect the timetables of others, particularly in commercial situations.

Dress appropriately.

Dress modestly and tastefully, particularly while visiting religious places or fancy eating establishments. Casual dress is allowed at beaches and marketplaces.

Try local cuisine.

Try local cuisine, including traditional and street food. St. Lucian food is a delicious combination of tastes that provides a one-of-a-kind culinary experience.

Use sun protection.

Protect yourself from the sun with sunscreen, a wide-brimmed hat, and sunglasses. The Caribbean heat may be intense, and sunburn can rapidly spoil your holiday.

Respect the environment.

St. Lucia's natural beauty is one of its most valuable assets. Avoid waste, protect coral reefs, and respect animal habitats.

Participate in water sports safely

Respect marine life and coral reefs while participating in water activities like snorkeling or scuba diving. Follow advice from guides and instructors to be safe.

Tipping

- ❖ Tipping is expected and appreciated in St. Lucia. In restaurants, a 10-15% gratuity is often added to the bill, although extra tips for outstanding service are appreciated.
- ❖ Recognize and reward tour guides, drivers, and hotel personnel for exceptional service.

Don'ts

Public displays of affection

Public expressions of love should be modest and respectful to local norms. Excessive or improper conduct may be regarded as offensive.

Disrespect local traditions.

Avoid mocking or disrespecting local customs, traditions, or religious practices. Show genuine interest and respect for St. Lucia's cultural Heritage.

Littering or damaging the environment

When snorkeling or diving, avoid littering, causing harm to coral reefs, or disturbing marine animals. Responsible tourism helps to maintain St. Lucia's natural beauty.

Overindulge in alcohol.

Enjoy the nightlife and local drinks, but avoid excessive alcohol consumption. Excessive drinking might result in undesirable consequences and health dangers.

Bargain aggressively.

Formal retail outlets seldom allow for bargaining. If you decide to negotiate, do it with dignity and a smile, particularly in rural marketplaces.

Photographing People Without Permission:

Ask permission before photographing individuals, particularly in rural or tiny areas. Respect their privacy and photographic preferences.

Engage in Illegal Activity

Illegal activities, including drug usage, are severely forbidden in St. Lucia. Violations may result in serious fines under local legislation.

Disrespecting wildlife

Avoid disturbing or harming animals, especially endangered species. Avoid feeding animals and keep a safe and respectful distance.

Ignore the Safety Guidelines

Follow safety standards and regulations, particularly for risky activities like hiking, zip-lining, and water sports. Your safety is crucial.

By following these dos and don'ts, you may improve your experience in St. Lucia and make great relationships with the locals. St. Lucians are famed for their warm hospitality, and your polite conduct will be met with genuine kindness and goodwill.

Responsible tourism guidelines.

St. Lucia's stunning landscapes, lush rainforests, and rich culture make it a natural and cultural wonderland. As a responsible visitor, you must participate in tourism activities that will conserve and maintain this Caribbean paradise for future generations. The following are complete rules for responsible tourism in St. Lucia:

Respect the environment.

Leave no trace

Experience St. Lucia's natural beauty while leaving no trace behind. Do not litter and properly dispose of your rubbish in designated containers.

Protect coral reefs

When snorkeling or diving, refrain from touching or destroying coral reefs. Keep safe from marine life and never touch or gather shells, corals, or other underwater objects.

Follow the Hiking Trails:

Use authorized hiking trails and follow established pathways. Do not develop new paths since they might destroy delicate ecosystems.

Reduce Plastic Use:

Reduce plastic waste by using reusable water bottles and bags. Many hotels and travel providers in St. Lucia promote environmentally friendly methods.

Support Local Communities:

Choose local products.

Buy locally produced crafts and souvenirs from craftsmen and marketplaces. This benefits local economies while preserving traditional handicrafts.

Dine Locally.

Experience authentic St. Lucian food at local restaurants and diners. Local cuisine supports the livelihoods of small-scale farmers and food producers.

Respect local culture.

Respect cultural customs and holidays. Before photographing individuals, particularly during religious or cultural activities, get their permission.

Learn about the culture.

Learn about St. Lucian culture, including history, customs, and traditions. Interacting with people and partaking in cultural activities promotes mutual respect and understanding.

Minimize your environmental footprint

Conserve water and energy.

Prioritize water and energy saving in your lodgings. Use towels and linens carefully, switch off unused lights and devices, and report any leaks or waste.

Use environmentally sustainable transportation.

Use eco-friendly transportation choices, such as public buses, shared shuttles, or walking. Alternatively, try hiring a bike or an electric car.

Support sustainable tourism initiatives:

Look for lodgings and tour providers certified for environmental practices. These firms are devoted to reducing their environmental effect.

Participate in conservation efforts.

Join Conservation Activities

Participate in local conservation initiatives like beach cleanups and tree planting events. Many organizations and resorts spearhead these programs.

Learn about local wildlife

Maintain a safe distance while witnessing wildlife. Learn about the local species and the significance of conserving their environment.

Follow Responsible Water Sports Practices.

Responsible Snorkelling and Diving

Select operators that prioritize reef conservation and appropriate engagement with marine animals.

Boating and Sail

When boating or sailing, adhere to maritime safety requirements and avoid anchoring in coral regions. Dispose of rubbish carefully, and avoid feeding animals.

Respect the regulations and laws.

Drug use

Drug usage is banned in St. Lucia, and offenders may face harsh penalties under local legislation.

Follow the National Park Rules

When visiting national parks or protected regions, follow park laws and regulations to preserve vulnerable ecosystems.

Responsible tourism in St. Lucia involves enjoying the island's beauty and helping preserve it. Following these detailed rules will help you have a good influence on the environment, assist local communities, and guarantee that St. Lucia remains a sustainable and treasured destination for future generations of guests.

Chapter 11: Itinerary.

One-Week Adventure in St. Lucia

St. Lucia, an exotic Caribbean Island noted for its stunning vistas, lush rainforests, and lively culture, provides the ideal environment for an amazing one-week vacation. Whether you like nature, adventure, or culture, St. Lucia offers something for everyone. Here's a carefully crafted one-week adventure schedule to help you maximize your stay in this tropical paradise.

Day One: Arrival in Castries.

• Arrive at Hewanorra International or George F. L. Charles Airport.

• Check in to your preferred accommodation in Castries, the capital city.

• Explore the city's history by strolling around Derek Walcott Square.

• Try St. Lucian food at a local eatery.

Day 2: Soufrière & Sulphur Springs

• Visit the lovely village of Soufrière on the west coast.

• Explore Sulphur Springs Park, the world's only drive-in volcano.

• Rejuvenate yourself with a mud bath in mineral-rich waters.

• Visit the neighbouring Diamond Falls and Botanical Gardens to see unique vegetation.

• Enjoy supper at a riverside restaurant with views of the Pitons.

Day 3: Piton Hike and Snorkeling

• Take a guided climb up Gros Piton, one of St. Lucia's famed twin peaks.

• Enjoy magnificent views of the island and Caribbean Sea from the peak.

• Reward yourself with a relaxing swim at Sugar Beach.

• Explore the colorful marine life in crystal-clear waters by snorkeling or scuba diving in the afternoon.

Day 4: Rainforest Adventures.

• Take a guided stroll through St. Lucia's beautiful rainforest at Edmund Forest Reserve.

• Explore secret waterfalls and learn about the island's unique flora and animals.

• Experience the excitement of zip-lining in a rainforest canopy adventure park.

• Enjoy a unique immersive experience by staying overnight in a rainforest eco-lodge.

Day 5: South Coast Exploration.

• Explore the gorgeous south coast, going through lovely fishing communities.

• Visit Anse Ivrogne for a quiet beach experience.

• Explore Vieux Fort's colonial architecture.

• Learn kite surfing at renowned Sandy Beach.

Day Six: Cultural Immersion

• Learn about St. Lucian culture at Fond Latisab Creole Park.

• Engage in traditional activities, sample local food, and enjoy live music.

• Explore the historic Pigeon Island National Landmark, with its ruins and beaches.

• Consider attending a local cultural event or festival during your vacation.

Day 7: Island Adventure and Farewell.

• Embark on a catamaran for a day of island hopping and snorkeling.

• Explore the Caribbean variety by visiting nearby islands such as Martinique and St. Vincent.

• Relax with a beach picnic and soak up the sun.

• Enjoy a goodbye meal in St. Lucia upon your return.

This one-week vacation in St. Lucia will make you appreciate the island's natural beauty, rich culture, and exciting outdoor activities. It's the ideal combination of leisure, discovery, and adventure, making your trip to St. Lucia an unforgettable experience.

Romantic getaway.

With its breathtaking surroundings, quiet beaches, and magnificent resorts, St. Lucia is the ideal romantic escape. Whether you're celebrating a honeymoon or an anniversary or just want to spend quality time with your loved one, St. Lucia is the ideal environment for romance. Here's how to organize an unforgettable romantic getaway on this fascinating Caribbean Island.

Choose your ideal accommodation

Luxury Resorts: St. Lucia has a variety of upmarket resorts, each with individual villas, infinity pools, and breathtaking ocean views. Consider selecting a private plunge pool room for a more intimate experience.

Boutique Hotels: Choose tiny boutique hotels in beautiful gardens or on cliffs overlooking the Caribbean Sea. These modest resorts often provide customized attention and romantic accents.

Overwater Bungalows: Some resorts include overwater bungalows, which enable you to wake up to the soft lapping of the waves and incomparable seclusion.

Treat yourself to spa treatments

Pamper yourself with couples' spa treatments located in peaceful, tropical settings. Many resorts include world-class spas with massages, facials, and wellness packages dedicated to couples. The serene setting and skilled therapists will heighten your sensation of relaxation and closeness.

Sunset Cruise

Go on a romantic sunset boat around St. Lucia's shore. Whether aboard a catamaran, sailboat, or private yacht, watching the sun set beyond the horizon while drinking champagne is a memorable experience. Some cruises feature meals and live music as an added touch of romance.

Explore the Natural Wonders

St. Lucia's natural splendour offers the ideal setting for romantic experiences.

- ❖ Hike Gros Piton or Petit Piton for stunning vistas and a shared feeling of achievement.
- ❖ Visit the Diamond Falls and Botanical Gardens for a peaceful romantic walk.
- ❖ jungle Canopy Tour: Enjoy zip-lining through the jungle while holding hands high above the trees.

Beach picnics

Spend a private beach picnic with your loved one. Many resorts provide this romantic experience, which includes a gourmet lunch, champagne, and a private place on the beach. Listen to the waves, see the stars, and make lifelong memories.

Sunset dinners

Dine at a beachside restaurant or on a cliffside patio while the sun sets over the Caribbean Sea. The balmy tropical wind, illuminated tables, and the sound of the waves create an incredibly romantic setting.

Cultural experiences

Attending local festivals, live music performances, or cultural presentations allows you to learn about the island's culture. Immerse yourself in St. Lucian culture, music, and dancing for an unforgettable evening together.

Adventure Together

Share thrilling activities like snorkeling, horseback riding, or exploring the island's gorgeous rainforests. These shared excursions will form enduring friendships and provide fascinating memories.

Private moments

Enjoy your exquisite accommodations in your suite, villa, or overwater bungalow. These quiet times, whether it's soaking in your hot tub, swimming at midnight, or stargazing from your balcony, are where memories are built.

Renew your vows

Consider renewing your vows in a romantic ceremony on the beach or in the beautiful garden. Many resorts provide vow renewal packages, which include a ceremony, a photographer, and a celebration supper.

A romantic trip in St. Lucia is a love festival set against the backdrop of the Caribbean's grandeur. Whether you're relishing the food, discovering the island's natural beauties, or enjoying each other's company, St. Lucia provides the ideal setting for an unforgettable love tale.

Chapter 12: Emergency Information

Medical Services

St. Lucia, like many nations, provides a variety of medical services to both inhabitants and tourists. While the island is best recognized as a vacation destination, it is critical to have access to trustworthy medical care in case of an unforeseen health issue. Here is a summary of the medical services and healthcare facilities available in St. Lucia:

Healthcare infrastructure

St. Lucia's healthcare system includes both governmental and private services. The overall quality of healthcare is high, with well-trained medical staff and sophisticated technology accessible. Some of the important healthcare facilities are:

- Victoria Hospital in Castries is St. Lucia's biggest public hospital, offering comprehensive medical services and specialized treatment.
- St. Jude Hospital in Vieux Fort provides healthcare services for the island's southern section.
- Private hospitals and clinics in St. Lucia, like Tapion Hospital, provide high-quality medical treatment for locals and visitors.

Medical Service

St. Lucia offers extensive medical services, which include:

- Emergency care is accessible at both public and private hospitals. Call 911 or go to the closest hospital in case of a medical emergency.
- The island offers several general practitioners (GPs) that provide primary healthcare services such as consultations, prescriptions, and basic treatments.
- Medical professionals such as surgeons, cardiologists, and gynecologists practice in St. Lucia and provide consultations and operations.
- Dentists on the island provide dental treatments, including check-ups, cleanings, and operations.
- Pharmacies: St. Lucia offers various pharmacies for prescriptions and over-the-counter drugs.
- Medical evacuation services are provided for extreme medical emergencies, transporting patients to specialist hospitals overseas.

Health Insurance

Travelers to St. Lucia should have adequate travel insurance that covers medical expenditures. Many hotels and resorts on the island demand customers to provide evidence of travel insurance when they check-in. St. Lucian inhabitants usually have access to the public healthcare system, which taxes support.

Vaccination and Health Precautions

It is suggested that you have standard vaccines before coming to St. Lucia and immunizations for illnesses such as hepatitis A and B, typhoid, and influenza. In addition, travelers should use insect repellent and protective clothes to avoid mosquito-borne diseases such as dengue and Zika.

Health & Safety

St. Lucia is typically a safe place for tourists. However, it is essential to maintain excellent hygiene and adhere to safety requirements, particularly regarding food and drink intake. Drinking bottled or filtered water is recommended.

St. Lucia provides various medical services and healthcare facilities to guarantee its people's and visitors' well-being. To have a safe and healthy stay on the island, ensure proper travel insurance and take health measures.

Emergency Contacts

When visiting or staying in St. Lucia, it is essential to know the emergency contact numbers for fast help in emergencies, accidents, or medical problems. The following are the major emergency contacts you should be aware of:

Emergency services

- To report a crime or accident or request police help, call 911. This is the universal emergency number for all police-related incidents.
- For fire or rescue emergencies, call 911.
- If you need medical help or an ambulance, call 911. Emergency medical services are sent using this number.

Hospitals and Medical Facilities

- Victoria Hospital, located in Castries, is the island's main public hospital. It offers extensive medical services and can be accessed at +1 758-452-2421.
- St. Jude Hospital, located in Vieux Fort, provides medical services for the southern region of St. Lucia. You may reach St. Jude Hospital at +1 758-454-6041.
- Private medical facilities in St. Lucia include Tapion Hospital in Castries. The contact information for these

institutions may differ, so keep the contact information for your preferred healthcare provider ready.

Embassy and Consulates

If you are a foreign traveler, you should have the contact information for your country's embassy or consulate in St. Lucia. They may aid with misplaced passports, legal concerns, and other consular services. Make sure you register with your embassy if necessary.

Coast Guard and Maritime Emergency

- For marine emergencies, such as boating accidents or trouble at sea, call the St. Lucia Coast Guard at +1 758-457-3186.

Roadside Assistance

If you have automobile difficulty or need roadside help, you may call a local towing and roadside assistance company. It is recommended.

Please be aware that although English is the official language of St. Lucia, local accents and dialects may differ. When making an emergency contact, explain clearly and simply about your location and facts to guarantee prompt and effective help.

These emergency contact numbers are critical for your safety and well-being when visiting or staying in St. Lucia. Whether you want medical aid, police involvement, or assistance in any other emergency scenario, having the proper contact numbers may make a big difference in quickly obtaining the care you need.

Chapter 13 covers practical information.

Currency and Money Matters

Understanding the currency, banking, and money concerns in St. Lucia is critical for a successful and happy visit to this lovely Caribbean Island. Here's a thorough resource to assist you with the financial elements of your trip:

Currency

St. Lucia's official currency is the Eastern Caribbean Dollar (XCD), which is symbolized by the sign "$" or the abbreviation "EC$." Because numerous Eastern Caribbean nations share the XCD, it is widely recognized in St. Lucia. It is also tied to the US dollar (USD) at a fixed rate of about 2.70 XCD to 1 USD.

Banking and ATMs

St. Lucia has a well-established financial system, with several banks and ATMs spread around the island. Some of the prominent banks are:

The Bank of St. Lucia has branches in Castries and Soufrière.

- First National Bank (FNB) has many branches in St. Lucia.

- Scotiabank, a member of the multinational Scotiabank network, provides financial services and operates many branches.
- RBC Royal Bank provides banking services in St. Lucia as an extension of the Royal Bank of Canada.

ATMs are widely distributed across towns, cities, and numerous resorts. Most ATMs accept major international credit and debit cards, such as Visa and MasterCard. It is best to notify your bank of your trip intentions to avoid card-related complications in St. Lucia.

Currency Exchange

Foreign cash may be exchanged for Eastern Caribbean Dollars at banks, currency exchange offices, and certain hotels and resorts. You may also locate local shops that take US dollars and other major foreign currencies for transactions. However, it is advisable to have some Eastern Caribbean Dollars on hand for minor transactions and in locations where US dollars may not be accepted.

Credit Cards

Credit cards are typically welcomed at the majority of hotels, dining establishments, retail establishments, and tourist destinations in St. Lucia. Visa and MasterCard are the most commonly used credit cards and are widely accepted. In some specific locations, American

Express and Discover cards may also be acknowledged. It is advisable to have some cash on hand for transactions in remote or smaller locations.

Traveler's checks

Traveler's checks were previously a prominent kind of cash among visitors, but their usage has substantially decreased. Nowadays, it is uncommon to locate places in St. Lucia that take traveler's checks. Credit and debit cards are more convenient for most financial transactions.

Tipping

Tipping is typical in St. Lucia and is appreciated for excellent service. A 10-15% service fee may be automatically applied to the bill in restaurants. It is normal to leave an extra tip for great service. When tipping taxi drivers, tour guides, and hotel workers, use the quality of service as a guideline for how much to offer.

Taxes and fees

- Value Added Tax (VAT): St. Lucia charges a 15% VAT on products and services, including meals at restaurants and lodgings. Consider this extra expense while planning your vacation.

- ❖ Departure tax is typically included in airline ticket prices. Check with your airline to see whether this cost is included or if you must pay it separately.

Currency Exchange Rates

The Eastern Caribbean Dollar's (XCD) exchange rate may vary against other major currencies, such as the US Dollar (USD). It's a good idea to check current exchange rates before traveling to St. Lucia, either via a bank or reputable internet sources, to get a sense of your money's worth.

By being acquainted with the currency and money concerns in St. Lucia, you may secure a stress-free and financially prudent vacation to this beautiful Caribbean location. Whether trying local cuisine, discovering natural marvels, or participating in recreational activities, having the correct financial information can improve your trip experience.

Photography Tips

St. Lucia's breathtaking scenery, lively culture, and abundant wildlife provide several picture possibilities. Whether you're a beginner or an experienced photographer, capturing the spirit of this Caribbean treasure may be a gratifying experience. Here are some photographic suggestions to help you get the most out of your St. Lucia photography adventures:

Golden Hour Magic

- The "golden hours," or soft, warm light at dawn and sunset, produce lovely and appealing lighting conditions. Plan your outdoor shots around these times to create stunning and dramatic photographs.
- To get famous photos of the Piton mountains, go to overlooks like the Tet Paul Nature Trail during golden hours for stunning silhouettes and colorful sky.

Scenic landscapes

- Use a wide-angle lens to capture the stunning scenery of St. Lucia. A wide-angle lens is ideal for capturing sweeping landscapes, lush jungles, and panoramic coastlines.
- Use foreground features like palm trees, boulders, or beach umbrellas to give depth and interest to your beach photos.

Cultural Encounters

- Capture photographs of nice locals. Before shooting photographs, ask for permission and attempt to capture genuine moments representing the island's rich culture.

- Attend local festivals, parades, and cultural events to capture vibrant traditions and festivities. Capture the bright clothes, dances, and music that distinguishes St. Lucia.

Wildlife Photography

- Bird Watching: St. Lucia is home to many bird species. Bring a zoom lens to get close-ups of beautiful birds like the St. Lucia Parrot and hummingbirds visiting tropical flowers.
- Use underwater cameras to photograph coral reefs, fish, and sea turtles when snorkeling or diving. Always respect aquatic life and employ responsible diving techniques.

Rainforest Adventure

- Explore the rainforests with macro photography to capture detailed details of tropical flora and animals, including brilliant blooms, exotic insects, and delicate orchids.
- When shooting waterfalls, use a tripod and moderate shutter speed to capture the smooth flow of water. Experiment with several perspectives to determine the most engaging composition.

Night Photography

- Astrophotography: St. Lucia's dark sky provides ideal conditions for astrophotography. Capture the Milky Way and stars above the Pitons for breathtaking nightscapes.

- Try long-exposure photographs of cityscapes or waterfronts to produce fantastical effects with light reflections on the water.

Safety and Respect

- Respect local traditions by asking permission before photographing individuals or holy locations. Be careful of cultural sensitivity and privacy.
- Prioritize environmental responsibility when shooting animals and natural environments. Avoid upsetting animals or sensitive habitats just to take a snapshot.

Gear and accessories

- Protect yourself from the tropical environment in St. Lucia by bringing rain covers and a UV filter for your camera.
- Carry backup batteries, memory cards, and cleaning materials to be prepared for unexpected situations.

Local Inspiration

- Consider attending local photography tours or seminars. Local guides may give information on hidden treasures and unique viewpoints.
- Inspire yourself by visiting local art galleries and craft markets featuring St. Lucian artists and craftsmen.

Share your story

- Keep a trip notebook to record your photography adventure. Include comments on the locales, people you've met, and the story behind your photographs.
- Share your St. Lucia experiences and images on social media platforms to connect with other visitors and photographers.

St. Lucia's natural beauty and colorful culture provide plenty of picture options. By following these photography recommendations and respecting local traditions and the environment, you may capture the soul of this breathtaking Caribbean paradise and create lasting memories with your camera.

Travel Apps

Traveling to a new place, such as St. Lucia, may be made easier and more fun by using numerous travel applications. These applications can help you plan your vacation, navigate the island, discover wonderful restaurants, and more. Here are some helpful travel applications for people visiting St. Lucia:

Google Maps

• Platforms: Android and iOS.

Google Maps is essential for navigating. It provides comprehensive maps, real-time traffic updates, public transit information, and the option to download maps for offline usage, which is useful in cases of poor connection.

WhatsApp

• Platforms: Android and iOS.

WhatsApp is a popular messaging program that connects users via text, phone, and video conversations. It may also be used to communicate with local contacts or tour providers.

XE Currency

• Platforms: Android and iOS.

XE Currency offers real-time exchange rates for the Eastern Caribbean Dollar (XCD) to help you convert and understand its worth in your currency.

TripAdvisor

• Platforms: Android and iOS.

TripAdvisor provides user-generated suggestions for hotels, restaurants, sights, and activities in St. Lucia. It's an excellent tool for arranging your trip and discovering the greatest spots to visit.

Weather.com

• Platforms: Android and iOS.

Use the Weather.com app to stay up-to-date on St. Lucia's weather conditions. It gives current weather predictions, including temperature, rainfall, and wind speed.

Duolingo

• Platforms: Android and iOS.

Duolingo is a language study program that can teach you basic French or Creole words, often spoken in St. Lucia. Learning a few native terms may improve your trip experience.

Google Translation

• Platforms: Android and iOS.

Google Translate translates text and audio from one language to another. It's great for getting over language difficulties and interacting with locals.

Uber or Lyft

• Platforms: Android and iOS.

Ride-sharing services may not be accessible in all locations of St. Lucia, although they may be useful for transportation in metropolitan areas such as Castries.

Yelp

• Platforms: Android and iOS.

Yelp offers reviews and ratings for restaurants, bars, and businesses in St. Lucia. It may help you find local eating alternatives and learn about other people's experiences.

Time Zone

Like many Caribbean islands, St. Lucia follows Atlantic Standard Time (AST) all year. St. Lucia's time zone does not follow Daylight Saving Time (DST); hence, when DST changes occur in other locations, the local time does not change.

- ❖ Standard Time: St. Lucia follows Atlantic Standard Time (AST), 4 hours behind Coordinated Universal Time (UTC-4). This implies that noon in St. Lucia corresponds to 4:00 PM Coordinated Universal Time (UTC).
- ❖ St. Lucia does not alter clocks for Daylight Saving Time (DST). This contrasts several other locations, which may transition to Atlantic Daylight Time (ADT) during the DST period (UTC-3).

Visitors visiting St. Lucia do not need to alter their watches or gadgets for time changes while traveling to or within the island since the country maintains a stable time zone all year. When planning foreign travel or activities during your stay in St. Lucia, remember the time zone difference.

Conclusion

As we complete our St. Lucia travel guide, we hope you have gained helpful insights, tips, and information to make your trip to this Caribbean paradise memorable. St. Lucia's natural beauty, unique culture, and friendly hospitality promise a voyage full of adventure, relaxation, and discovery.

St. Lucia has a wide selection of activities and experiences to fit any traveler's interests, from the renowned Piton mountains and stunning beaches to the lush rainforests and active local customs. Whether you're looking for romantic vacations, exciting excursions, or cultural immersions, this island offers something for everyone.

Remember to immerse yourself in the local culture, interact with the friendly St. Lucians, and enjoy the island's exquisite food. Explore hidden jewels, participate in exhilarating water sports, and learn about this lovely place's rich history.

As you embark on your St. Lucian vacation, appreciate the natural marvels, respect the environment, and create memorable moments with your camera. Use the suggested travel apps to make your trip more enjoyable and easy.

St. Lucia calls with its unique allure, and we invite you to embrace the magic of this Caribbean treasure. Whether relaxing on a golden beach, trekking through verdant rainforests, or immersing yourself in local culture, St. Lucia will surely make an unforgettable impression on your spirit.

Thank you for picking this travel guide as your St. Lucia companion. May your trip be one of pleasure, discovery, and perfect happiness. Have a safe trip, and may you make memories that last a lifetime on this gorgeous island.

Bonus: Travel Budget Planner & Travel Journal

TRAVEL BUDGET PLANNER

DESTINATION: ____________________ TRAVEL DATES: ____________________

TRANSPORTATION	BUDGETED	ACTUAL
AIRFARE	$	$
AIRPORT PARKING	$	$
CHECKED LUGGAGE	$	$
CAR RENTAL	$	$
BUS / TAXI / TRANSIT / TRAIN	$	$
TOTAL	$	$

ACCOMMODATION	BUDGETED	ACTUAL
HOTEL/ AIR BNB	$	$
PARKING	$	$
MISCELLANEOUS COSTS	$	$
TOTAL	$	$

FOOD & DRINK	BUDGETED	ACTUAL
RESTAURANTS	$	$
SNACKS	$	$
COFFEE & TEA	$	$
GROCERIES	$	$
TOTAL	$	$

ENTERTAINMENT	BUDGETED	ACTUAL
ORGANIZED TOURS	$	$
SIGHTSEEING & ATTRACTIONS	$	$
NIGHTLIFE	$	$
SPA TREATMENTS	$	$
SHOPPING	$	$
MISCELLANEOUS	$	$
TOTAL	$	$

OTHER EXPENSES	BUDGETED	ACTUAL
TRAVEL INSURANCE	$	$
PASSPORT, VISA, DOCUMENTS	$	$
VACCINATIONS & MEDICATIONS	$	$
MOBILE PHONE FEES	$	$
CURRENCY EXCHANGE	$	$
MISCELLANEOUS COSTS	$	$
TOTAL	$	$
GRAND TOTAL	$	$

TRAVEL

DATE:

DURATION:

DESTINATION:

PLACES TO SEE:

1
2
3
4
5
6
7

LOCAL FOOD TO TRY:

1
2
3
4
5
6
7

DAY 1

DAY 2

DAY 3

DAY 4

DAY 5

DAY 6

NOTES

EXPENSES IN TOTAL:

PLANNER

TRAVEL

DATE:

DURATION:

DESTINATION:

PLACES TO SEE:

1
2
3
4
5
6
7

LOCAL FOOD TO TRY:

1
2
3
4
5
6
7

DAY 1

DAY 2

DAY 3

DAY 4

DAY 5

DAY 6

NOTES

EXPENSES IN TOTAL:

PLANNER

TRAVEL

DATE:
DURATION:

DESTINATION:

PLACES TO SEE:	LOCAL FOOD TO TRY:
1	1
2	2
3	3
4	4
5	5
6	6
7	7

DAY 1	DAY 2	DAY 3

DAY 4	DAY 5	DAY 6

NOTES	EXPENSES IN TOTAL:

PLANNER

Notes

Notes

Notes

Notes

Made in the USA
Las Vegas, NV
17 October 2024

97018281R00115